MW01611725

Summer Days with the Moodys

by Sarah Maxwell

illustrated by Abigail Klein

 Communication Concepts, Inc.

Summer Days with the Moodys

Copyright © 2009 by Communication Concepts, Inc.

All rights reserved. Written permission must be secured from the publisher to use or reproduce any part of this book except for brief quotation in critical reviews or articles.

Ordering information:

Managers of Their Homes
1504 Santa Fe Street
Leavenworth, Kansas 66048
Phone: (913) 772-0392
Web site: www.Titus2.com

Published by:

Communication Concepts, Inc.
Web site: www.we-communicate.com

ACKNOWLEDGMENTS

Scripture taken from the HOLY BIBLE, KING JAMES VERSION.

ISBN 978-0-9771420-9-5

Printed in the United States of America.

1

This book was created in Microsoft Word. QuarkXPress 6 and Adobe Photoshop were used for layout and design. All computers were Windows-based systems running Windows XP/2000.

Christopher Maxwell designed the cover, and Sarah Maxwell designed the interior of this book. Abigail Klein drew the illustrations.

This book is dedicated to:

My family

Without you all, this book wouldn't be here! Thank you,
Dad, Mom, Christopher, Joseph, John,
Anna, Jesse, and Mary. I love you all!

Contents

Preface

I am deeply grateful to my family for all the help they have offered. They invested countless hours listening and offering many suggestions. It's not lightly stated that the book would not be what it is without them. A special thanks to Anna and Mary who were my own "sister editors," and also Dad and Mom for all their editing! My parents' encouragement helped me keep going when discouragement set in. Because this is the fifth book in the series, keeping track of details and remaining true to previously stated events and descriptions made consistency more difficult.

Five families "tested" the book and gave comments for the back cover. Thank you for your help! Another "thank you" to the families who helped with some of the photos used for the sketches. Our faithful, professional proofreader "scrubbed" the book.

I'm grateful to Abi who spent many hours drawing the sketches for *Summer Days*. What a great job you did!

My desire through the Moody Family Series is for children to be spurred on to obedience to their parents, to have sweet relationships with their brothers and sisters, and most importantly, to know Jesus Christ as their Lord and Savior. May the Moodys be the Lord's instrument!

Serving Jesus,
Sarah Maxwell

Meet the Characters

Mr. Moody—Dad (Jim) is the happy father of six children. He works at a bank. When he has fulfilled his duties at work, his preferred place is at home, spending time with his family. His heart's desire is to be a man of God and the spiritual leader of his family.

Mrs. Moody—Mom (Emily) is a homeschooling, stay-at-home mom. She dearly loves being a helpmeet to her husband and mother to her six children.

Max—Max (Maxwell), twelve, enjoys being the oldest child. Max has a heart for the Lord and wants to please Him.

Mollie—Mollie, ten, is a happy young lady. She loves Jesus and looks for ways to bless others.

Mitch—Mitch (Mitchell), nine, tends to have a unique suggestion or comment for the situation at hand. He makes his time in God's Word a priority each day.

Maddie—Four-year-old Madelynn, affectionately known as Maddie, loves being a big sister to the Moody twins. Her cute comments and view of life add a spark to the Moody household.

Moses and Melissa—The little Moody twins are such a joy, and they lend an extra special sparkle to life.

Grandpa and Grandma—James and Martha are Dad's parents, and both recently accepted the Lord as their Savior.

Grandma Clifton—Mrs. Clifton is an elderly widow whom the Moodys have helped and also the owner of Honey, a golden retriever.

Mrs. Maud Bagwell—Mrs. Bagwell lives up the street from the Moodys.

Mr. Delome—Mr. Delome is the Moodys' neighbor who lives across the street. He recently accepted the Lord Jesus as his Savior.

Mr. and Mrs. Parker—A young couple from the Moodys' church who is helping them with the church services at the nursing home.

National Pastor—The Moodys support a national pastor in Zambia. If you would like to know more about national pastors and how you may support them, visit this site: www.FamiliesforJesus.com/pastors

Mr. Gibson—The animal "catcher"! The Moodys have developed a friendship with him, and they enjoy seeing him as opportunities arise.

Mr. and Mrs. Russell—They are friends of the Moody family and owners of Peaches, the cat, whom the Moody children pet-sat last summer. Their baby, Madison, is a little older than the twins.

Background

The Moody family lives in a city called Sunflower, nestled among the rolling hills of eastern Kansas. They have six children, the youngest of whom are twins, and have been homeschooling since Max was in preschool. Even though Dad currently works at a bank, his desire is that he might someday have a business with his sons working from home. The family is just beginning a ministry holding Sunday morning services at a local nursing home.

Come join the Moodys for the summer!

Chapter

1

The Storm

Max was startled awake. As his sleepy mind tried to figure out what had roused him, he was aware of something pressing firmly against him. A flash of light illuminated the room, and he could see Maple's paw gripping his right arm as she half stood next to his bed. Maple was the Moodys' almost one-year-old golden retriever, and she was terrified of storms. A pitiful squeak came from Maple as a rumble of thunder echoed outside. "Okay," Max whispered permission. "You may get on my bed." Twelve-year-old Max slept on the bottom bunk, and Mitch, his nine-year-old brother, had the top one.

Max reached out to pat the frantic dog, but his only reward was a handful of wet slobber. *She really IS upset,* he thought. Max felt for his flashlight, and his fingers found the cool, metal object. Leaving Maple on the bed, he slipped from the room to wash his hands and get a drink of water. He was glad for the nightlight in the bathroom so he didn't have to turn on the main light. Max used a small amount of soap and then thoroughly rinsed his hands. After satisfying his thirst, he went back to his room. As he softly closed the door, several flashes of lightning lit up the room. Maple was still standing on the bed, panting and shaking.

I guess I'll work on my Scripture memory since this storm will probably last a while, and I'll be awake with Maple, he thought to himself. For several minutes, Max silently reviewed Colossians 3 as he tried to calm the panic-stricken dog by patting her. A bright flash of lightning was instantly followed by two more. Max remembered he could determine how far the strike was by counting the seconds between the flash and the thunder, then dividing by five: *one, two, three, four, five, six, seven, eight.* The thunder rumbled at that moment, and the rain sounded louder. *I think it was about a mile and a half away.*

"Max," Mitch announced in a sleepy voice. "The storm woke me up, and I can feel our bed shaking. Did you let Maple get on the bed?"

"Yes, she wanted to. At least you were able to sleep a little longer than I did; Maple woke me up about ten minutes ago by putting her paw on my arm. I knew she'd be upset for a while and that going back to sleep wasn't an option, so I'm reviewing my memory verses," Max responded.

Mitch threw off his sheet and clambered down the ladder two rungs at a time. He padded over to the window, knelt down, and raised the blind a few inches. "What does it look like?" Max asked Mitch.

"It's pouring rain and very windy. I hope it doesn't hail because I think Dad may have left the van out." Mitch couldn't tell if their twelve-passenger van was parked in the driveway. "Wow! It's really lightning!" Mitch quickly dropped the blind. "It's not good to be near a window when lightning strikes," Mitch remembered, "so I'll stay away from it."

"You're right," Max agreed. "By the way, I heard Dad pull the van in as I was going to sleep."

"Good." Mitch sat on the floor next to Max's bed. "Could you try to get Maple off the bed? Maybe I could go back to sleep then."

"That's a hopeless cause," Max whispered. "She won't budge."

As the boys listened to the storm, there was an almost constant rumble of thunder. The rain picked up, and then a brilliant flash of light, followed by a close crash of thunder, caused Max and Mitch to jump. "Now that must have been close," Max gasped.

"I know," Mitch agreed. "I'm surprised it didn't take out our electricity!"

A soft knock was heard, and ten-year-old Mollie poked her head in the room. "I was thirsty—it must have been that pizza last night—and I heard whispering in here. Are you guys talking about the storm?"

"We are," Mitch answered. "Maple sure has her storm brains working right now; she is on Max's bed, all upset."

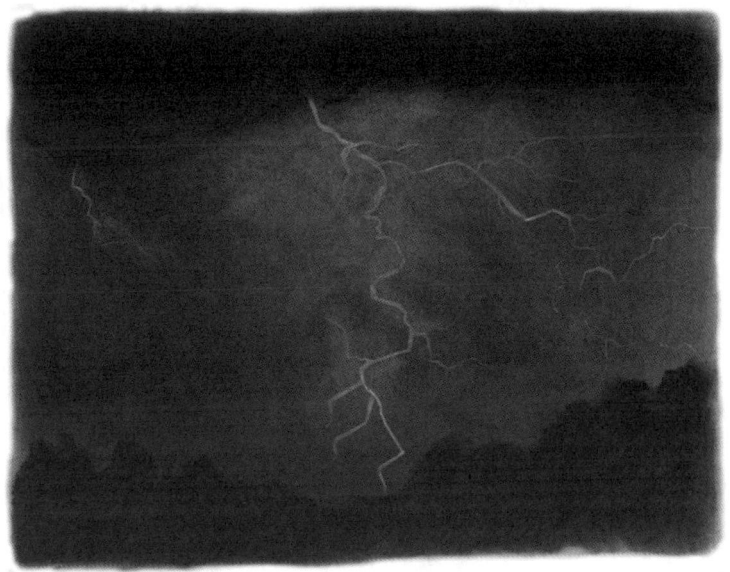

"Wow! It's really lightning!" Mitch quickly dropped the blind.

Another bright flash lit up the room, and rain began hitting the window. "I wonder if the wind changed directions," Mollie remarked, standing in the doorway. "I hadn't been hearing it on the window, but now I just started to. I'd better get back to bed in case Maddie wakes up." Four-year-old Maddie shared a room with Mollie. Mollie slipped into her bed, and as she pulled the sheet over her shoulders, a crash of thunder shook the house.

"I'm scared." Maddie's voice trembled as she was finally wakened by the storm. She scrambled from her bed and climbed into Mollie's. "I don't like thunder."

"I know you don't, but remember how storms remind us of God's power. When it storms, Mom encourages us to think about how grateful we are for our house and that we don't have to be outside." The lightning became more frequent, and there seemed no end to the continual thunder. Mollie thought she heard a new rumble of thunder beginning, but then a lump caught in her throat: it was the distinct, shrill whine of the tornado sirens!

Maddie gripped Mollie's arm tightly. "What's that?"

Before Mollie could respond, Mitch's shout was heard: "It's the tornado sirens! Hurry, we need to get downstairs!" He flipped on the hallway light, flung open the girls' door, turned to Dad and Mom's room, and pounded on their door. "Dad! Mom! The tornado sirens are going off!"

"Thanks, Mitch. We hear them," a voice responded, and there were several thuds as Dad and Mom's feet hit the floor. "Emily, grab what you need for the twins," Dad's muffled voice urged, and he opened the door. "Children, quickly get some clothes and a pair of shoes. Then go to the basement. We will be down as soon as we gather a few things for the twins." The almost twelve-week-old Moody twins, Moses and Melissa, shared a crib in Dad and Mom's room.

"Yes, sir."

By now, Max had the bedroom light on, and he was rummaging through dresser drawers. "If the tornado does come through," Mitch told Max, "we'll be able to escape the rubble with shoes and normal clothes, not just socks and pajamas!"

"I almost have what I need," Max said.

Mitch frantically dug through the closet, and his pajama pants pockets were soon bulging. "What are you doing?" Max turned away from the dresser. "We don't have much time, and I need to get my jeans and shoes from there!"

"I'm getting more stuff. I need my flashlight, a letter Dad wrote me after I got saved, and things like my birthday money. If the house is ruined, we'll need money. I almost forgot tracts. Dad has told me that after a disaster, people are more open to spiritual things. I think I have it all: let's go!"

Dad's voice called, "It doesn't sound like you all are downstairs; you need to hurry."

"Yes, sir," Max responded, grabbing his needed items. He glanced over and saw Maple had moved from the bed to the middle of the room. She was still panting and shaking. "Maple, come," Max firmly commanded the almost-crazy dog.

Mollie and Maddie were going by their door just then, and Maddie clutched her doll, Abigail. Stopping in the middle of the hall, Maddie's eyes fastened on Mitch's thick pockets. Mollie tugged on her hand. "Come on, Maddie! Dad said we must hurry!"

As they rushed down the stairs, a roaring sound was heard. "Is that hail?" Mitch shouted.

"Probably," Max agreed. "But we can't stop to look; we have to keep moving!"

Mitch turned on several lights as they trooped down the stairs to the basement. "Where's our weather radio?" Mitch asked as he rummaged around on a tall set of metal shelves near the stairs. "Here it is. I hope there are batteries in it."

Just then, Dad and Mom joined them with the twins. Melissa's brown eyes squinted in the light as she looked solemnly at Max. An old blue sofa and several chairs were the extent of the furniture in that area of the basement, so Max scooted the chairs nearer to the sofa to make a semicircle. Mom sank onto the couch, and she smiled. "We're all here! I'm glad we have water and supplies in the basement— this was the first time I didn't have to grab things from the pantry in case we need them. Dad had a great idea to have a little emergency-preparedness stash down here."

"It was from the Lord," Dad agreed. "Let's listen to what the weather radio is saying." Moses began crying so Mom found his binky in the diaper bag. Maddie quickly claimed a spot next to Mom and snuggled close.

The radio crackled as Mitch turned up the volume: "This is your National Weather Service. At 1:13 a.m., trained weather spotters reported a funnel cloud in a severe thunderstorm in Leawood County moving northeast at approximately 30 miles per hour. A tornado warning is in effect for the following counties: Leawood, Sunflower, and Plattener. Remember, a tornado warning is serious, and it is important to find shelter immediately. Always keep food, water, blankets, and a flashlight available and expect the worst. The storm is expected to be in Sunflower at 1:37 a.m. and Plattener at 1:50 a.m. Always stay alert when conditions are uncertain."

"A storm that might have a tornado is headed this way!" Mitch exclaimed.

Mollie thought about their elderly neighbor, the widow Grandma Clifton, and her golden retriever, Honey. "Dad, do you think Grandma Clifton's okay?"

"I expect so. She knows to go to the basement." Dad reached down and patted Maple. She was lying near Dad, sides heaving from panting and head cocked to listen for another crash of thunder. "I'll call Grandma Clifton to make sure— that is, if I have her number in my phone." Dad pulled his cell phone from his pocket and scrolled through the list of numbers on his phone. "Found it." Grandma Clifton answered, and they talked for a minute before Dad reported: "She's in her basement with Honey, and they're fine."

Mitch passed the radio to Max and said, "You may have a turn. What's the radio saying now?" When Mitch was excited, he was always full of comments and questions.

"I don't know," answered Max. He held the radio to his ear because Melissa was fussing. "Let me listen for a minute . . . It's awfully crackly sounding, but from what I can understand, the tornado is still headed in our direction, and it hasn't touched ground." Max nervously looked at Dad.

"Did they say what kind it is?" Mitch wondered.

"What kind?" Max repeated.

"Yes, like if it's an F1, F2, or F3. If an F2 hits our house, the roof will be torn off, trees will be snapped, and lots of stuff will be blown through the air." Mitch was glad to share his knowledge of tornadoes. "On the other hand, if it's an F3, our house would be totally—"

"Mitch!" Dad shook his head as Maddie's lip started to quiver. "We don't need to go through all the details. There's no reason to frighten Maddie."

"Yes, sir. I was remembering what I read in my science book."

"I'm glad you've retained that information, but we don't want to worry others. Let's take a few minutes to pray for the Lord's protection on our city. Whoever wants to may pray. I'll start. Dear Heavenly Father, thank You for the blessing of a home. I'm also grateful for this family You have given me. I pray that You would protect Sunflower and all the surrounding areas from the tornado. Truly, You are in control of the weather, and we pray Your hand would keep the tornado from touching down. We know we don't deserve Your mercy, yet we humbly ask You to protect everyone. Please help the storm to pass quickly. In Jesus' Name."

Maddie peeked around the circle and whispered to Mom, "I'll go next. Dear Jesus, thank You for my home, and for my daddy and mommy and my brothers and sisters and for Maple. Please help that tornado to go far, far away. Amen."

After the family finished praying, Dad's cell phone rang, and he glanced at the Caller ID. "It's Grandpa." After a short conversation, Dad stuck his phone in his pocket. "Grandpa and Grandma are fine: they're enjoying a little snack in their basement. They also just finished a time of prayer."

Melissa yawned and reached for Dad's face. In return, Dad smiled and tickled her. "I guess that's not the best thing to do if Mom wants them to go back to sleep," he said to Mom.

Maddie snuggled closer to Mom. "I don't like storms."

There was a house-shaking crash, and everything went dark. Even from the basement, they could hear wind fiercely blowing. Melissa began to cry, and Moses joined her. Mitch switched on his flashlight. "Don't worry! I have us covered!" With that, he shone the light toward Dad.

Dad shielded Melissa's eyes from the light. "You can point it away from us. I know we have another flashlight under the stairs."

Mitch scurried over to the stairs, and there was some rustling as he searched for the light. "Found it!" A bright beam of light shone directly in Dad's eyes.

"Yes, but I'm seeing stars now!" Dad chuckled.

"Sorry."

Several minutes passed, and the lights came back on. "That's wonderful," Dad said. "They weren't off for too long. It's 1:46. Max, why don't you turn up the weather radio volume, and we'll see what they have to say."

The nasal-sounding voice crackled over the radio: "The tornado warning for Sunflower County was cancelled as of 1:43 a.m. The storm is no longer a threat to Sunflower County. Repeating, the tornado warning for Sunflower County is cancelled, message 101."

Mitch sighed. "I'm sad. I thought maybe a tornado would hit near here! I've never seen a real live one."

Dad shook his head. "You don't understand. Tornadoes are serious, and they can do lots of property damage. I'm praising the Lord for His protection. Time for bed!"

Chapter 2

Dad's Idea

Glancing at the clock, Mollie was startled that it was so late. Light streamed in through the edges of her blind. Putting on her robe, she slipped quietly from the room. Mom's door was open; she sat on the bed reading her Bible, and the twins were asleep in the crib. "Good morning, Mollie. Did you sleep well?" she whispered.

"I was so tired after being up with the storm that I didn't roll over all the rest of the night. Would you like me to wake Maddie?"

"Yes, we should get started on our day. We'll have breakfast at 8:45. That should give you all plenty of time to read your Bibles, pray, and get dressed. I'm going to wake the boys now."

An hour later, Max, Mollie, Mitch, and Maddie came downstairs and found Dad in the living room. He looked up from his Bible: "Good morning, children!"

"Are you going to work today?" Mitch knew Dad usually left for work much earlier than this.

"I'll tell you about it at breakfast," Dad said mysteriously, closing his Bible.

Maddie spotted Moses on a blanket near Dad, so she dropped to her knees, picked up a rattle, and waved it in front of the baby. She kissed his forehead. "I love you, Moses."

"Time to eat!" Mom called.

Maddie gave Moses one more kiss before Dad scooped him up. He buckled Moses into the baby swing Grandpa and Grandma had given them recently as a gift; it made mealtimes much simpler with one of the twins happy in the swing while the other was in Mom's sling or being held.

"Max, would you please get the loaf of bread from the counter?" Mom requested. "I forgot it."

"Yes, ma'am."

Dad brought the toaster from the kitchen, placed it in the middle of the table, and plugged it into an extension cord, which reached a nearby wall outlet. "Melissa sure looks cute in the sling."

Mom smiled. "It was your gift! I was so blessed by the baby shower the children gave before the twins were born." Mom put four slices of bread into the toaster so they could begin toasting.

"The shower was all their planning," Dad replied, "and that made it just that much more special. Max, you may bless the food."

"Dear Jesus, we're grateful for a calm day after the storm. Thank You for Your protection of our house. Help Dad to get a lot of work done if he's going to work, or if he's not, whatever we do. Please bless this food. In Jesus' Name, Amen."

Dad dumped a spoonful of juicy pineapple pieces onto his plate. "Now I'll answer your question from earlier, Mitch. I'm not going into work."

"Why not?" Mitch wondered.

"My boss called, and the electricity is out at the bank; they're hoping it'll be working by noon. He said to enjoy a day off."

"Splendid," Mitch responded as the toast popped up. He took a piece, buttered it, and squeezed a generous amount of honey over the surface of the toast. "There's one positive thing about the storm."

"I have a plan for this morning." Dad glanced at the children's faces to make sure he had their attention. "When I talked to my boss, he said he'd seen on the news that the wind gusts in Sunflower were sixty miles per hour, which led to much tree damage. We're going to drive around to see if we can find somebody who needs help with storm cleanup."

"I like that!" Mitch blurted. "We could be D-A-R! Disaster Assistance Relief!"

"I can't wait!" Mollie was excited.

Dad chuckled. "Good idea, Mitch, but let's see if we can come up with a name that honors Jesus. You know the verse that says if you give a cup of cold water in My Name? . . . Hmmm. How about I-J-N? In Jesus' Name."

"Perfect," Mitch agreed.

Discussion about the storm continued during breakfast. When the last bite was finished, Dad was ready to move on. "Okay, I-J-N team. Mom will feed the twins, and we'll take care of the breakfast dishes, although there isn't much. I know everyone is dressed for the day, but I think a nice touch to our outing would be to wear uniforms. It adds a sharp look to companies in the business world. Let's see: who has a red shirt?"

"Uniforms?" Mitch's eager voice spoke. "We'd really look official!"

There was a bit of debate until it was confirmed they all had red shirts. "Then the dress code," Dad announced, "will be red with denim. Red shirts plus denim jumpers or jeans. I know you still have room chores to accomplish, so do those, then meet me in the garage to gather up our I-J-N tools!"

The children swung into fast motion, and breakfast cleanup was done swiftly. They rushed to change into their uniforms and complete their chores. Maddie perched on the edge of her bed while Mollie worked on combing Maddie's hair.

"Your hair isn't as curly as it used to be. Mom said my hair was like yours until I was four, and then it became straight. Do you want a ponytail?" Mollie asked.

"Yes, and please make it tight. Mollie, when is Melissa going to sleep in our room?"

"I don't know; Dad says we need to buy another crib before Melissa can move since we only have one."

When Max and Mitch were ready, they hurried down to the garage. "You boys look sharp," complimented Dad. "Mitch, please find a roll of trash bags. Max, I think we'll need a few rakes, which are probably in the basement."

Just then, the girls burst into the garage: "Look, Daddy; we're matching!" Maddie showed Dad her denim jumper.

"You both look like part of the I-J-N team," Dad affirmed as he pulled two pairs of small hedge clippers off of a peg board. "We'll probably have a use for these."

"Dad," Mollie began, "I know where the gloves are."

"You and Maddie may get them and put them in a bag so we don't lose them. We might have some other items for the bag before we leave."

The girls located several pairs of work gloves and put them in a canvas tote bag. Meanwhile, Mitch stuffed trash bags into the back of the van. "A shovel might be handy, especially if we come across piles of dirt or something," Mitch suggested, showing Dad a long-handled shovel.

Dad patted Mitch on the back. "Go for it. Also, grab a roll of twine. We may need it to bundle sticks together."

Max brought two rakes, and Dad slid them in along the van floor. "The next step is to identify our team," Dad said. He found a roll of blue masking tape. "I guess we'll need a pair of scissors."

Max felt in his pocket and pulled out a shiny, silver pocketknife. "Dad, I have my pocketknife, and we could use that to cut the tape!"

"Perfect," Dad responded.

"What are you doing?" Mitch was puzzled.

"We're going to use the tape to form our I-J-N initials on the side of the van." Dad let Max cut three strips of tape, and Dad worked on creating the letter "I."

After several minutes, I-J-N was boldly displayed. "That should do," Dad decided. "Your pocketknife worked great, Max. I'll see if Mom and the twins are ready. In the meantime, please load the stroller into the back of the van; it'll be a tight fit with our tools, but I think you can manage."

Soon, everyone was buckled in—the adventure was at hand! Excited chatter began while Dad backed from the garage. "There's Mr. Delome," Mitch said. Mr. Delome lived across the street from the Moodys, and he had recently accepted the Lord as his Savior.

Dad pulled into Mr. Delome's driveway and rolled his window down. "Good morning!"

"Howdy," Mr. Delome answered. He was dressed in a work outfit of faded jeans and a long-sleeve T-shirt, both of which had seen better days. *The one thing he is missing,* Mitch thought, *is work boots.* Instead, he wore white socks with sandals.

"You obviously survived the storm," Dad stated, shutting off the engine.

"Yes; I'm grateful there are no limbs down, just a lot of small sticks."

"Do you need help?" Dad asked. Without waiting for a response, the children piled from the van, and they rushed to work on Mr. Delome's front yard.

Mr. Delome laughed. "What are they doing?"

"Did you look at the side of the van?"

"Come on, Jim. Why should I look at the side of your van?" He turned to scrutinize it. "I-J-N. Is that a secret code?"

"Sort of: it stands for In Jesus' Name. We're going to see if we can find anyone who needs help cleaning up after the storm, and we're doing it in Jesus' Name. Electricity is out at the bank, so my boss said I can have the day off."

"That's a nice plan." Mr. Delome smiled; there was silence for a minute, but then the rumble of a motor was heard, and Mr. Delome turned to see an old truck pull up near the curb. "If it isn't Rob Coppen, my friend! You should come meet him, Jim."

Dad climbed from the van and looked curiously in the direction of the truck. A short, stocky man, with a gray mustache and hair that slightly escaped from a ball cap, jumped out and greeted Mr. Delome: "Howdy, Lomers." He gave Mr. Delome a hearty handshake and nodded at Dad. "I was in this part of town, and I wanted to check on you. I'm never too busy to help a friend. Do you need me to haul anything away?"

"I think I'm set, Rob," Mr. Delome decided. "I really appreciate you stopping by. While you're here, I want you to meet Jim Moody. His fine children are working on my yard."

"Pleased to meet you," Mr. Coppen said before hurrying back to his truck. "I've got to be running."

Mr. Delome tried to delay Mr. Coppen. "So you keeping busy?"

"Always, always. Everyone needs me! There's a lot of work around town to be done, and my phone is ringing all the time. So long, Lomers!" With a wave, Mr. Coppen abruptly left.

For the first time, Dad noticed a man sitting in the passenger seat of Mr. Coppen's truck. He appeared to be a small, thin man with a dark tan. Mr. Delome turned to Dad. "The guy with him is Joe. He works for Rob, and they are two peas in a pod." He rubbed his beard and turned his attention back to the children. "I wish I'd taught Bill, when he was growing up, to have the sort of attitude you're teaching your children about work. But, you all need to get on your way; time's a wasting. It won't take me long to get the rest of the yard picked up: the children have already made splendid progress. Besides, it's good exercise for me!"

"Then we'll be off."

"By the way," Mr. Delome added, "would you like to borrow my chainsaw?"

"I hadn't thought of that, but yes, we would."

"I'll be glad for it to get some use," Mr. Delome said. "I'll send along the gas too."

"Thank you," Dad said. "Moody children! Let's move along to find others who might need help. Mr. Delome says he will finish his yard himself. We're going to borrow his chainsaw, though, so Max, would you please try to squeeze it in the back?"

"Come on, Jim. Why should I look at the side of your van?"
He turned to scrutinize it. "I-J-N. Is that a secret code?"

"Yes, sir."

Dad opened the door to talk to Mom. "I'll run over to our garage to get safety glasses and ear protectors in the event we use the chainsaw."

Soon, the family was on their way. "I was having fun helping Mr. Delome. Hopefully we'll find someone with lots of damage." Mitch strained to look around Max. "That yard's a mess. Too bad people are cleaning it up."

They all watched for a place to stop as Dad drove slowly through a nearby neighborhood. "There's one!" Mollie called, noticing a middle-aged couple working in a yard. Dad parked the van in the street.

Max popped open his window to listen to the conversation. "Hello!" Dad greeted the couple as he walked up. "Looks like you have a bit of work ahead of you."

"Sure do." The man took off his glasses, polishing them with a well-worn handkerchief. "My son is coming over soon to lend us a hand."

"My family and I would love to help you with cleanup if you need it."

The man shook his head. "Thanks for the offer, but we're taken care of."

After Dad climbed in the van, Max seemed slightly discouraged. "Dad, maybe the I-J-N on the van is hindering us."

"I'm sure that's not the problem; it appears either we have industrious people in Sunflower, or we haven't come to an area that was hard hit. We'll keep driving for a while, and see if we can find someone to help."

Chapter
3

A Team Effort

Several minutes later, the Moodys drove down a tree-lined street, with older houses on each side of the road. "Wait, Dad! Look over there!" Mitch exclaimed, pointing to the right. "I see a lady working by herself."

The small, elderly lady with a sun visor over her curly gray hair walked with a slight limp. In the middle of the yard, a medium-size Bradford pear tree was split down the middle, and half of the tree rested on the ground. Many smaller branches were scattered across the yard. Dad pulled the van into the driveway and hopped out. The lady quit working when she saw him and called, "Hello!"

"Good morning," Dad responded. "It looks like you have quite a mess in your yard, and my family wants to help someone with their storm cleanup. You seem like a possible candidate."

"How much are you charging?"

"Nothing—we'd just like to help."

The lady's face brightened. "I can't tell you how blessed I would be. I've had two tree companies come by, but they wanted an unreasonable amount to take down the tree. I knew the Lord would provide a way. Oh, here I go rambling: I'm Lucille Hayden."

"I'm Jim Moody, and we live over on Strawberry Lane. I'd like for you to meet my family." Mrs. Hayden followed Dad to the vehicle. "Mrs. Hayden, this is my wife, Emily." Dad opened the door for Mom.

Mrs. Hayden clasped Mom's hand in hers. "I'm pleased to meet you."

"I'm Mitch." Mitch shook her hand.

"He's the third oldest," Dad said. "Our first-born is Max."

Max smiled at Mrs. Hayden. "Hello."

"I'm Mollie."

"Don't forget me! I'm Madelyn." Leaping from the van, Maddie landed in the soft grass. "But you can call me Maddie if you prefer."

"How many children do you have?" Mrs. Hayden asked Mom.

"Six; the youngest are twins: Moses and Melissa."

Max unloaded the stroller while Mitch worked on unpacking the supplies they would need. Mrs. Hayden noticed the blue lettering on the side of the van. "I'm curious: what does I-J-N stand for?"

Mitch promptly answered, "In Jesus' Name!"

"Sounds to me like you are Christians. I have been a believer for many years."

"Yes." Dad buckled Moses into the stroller. "We are Christians saved by the blood of Jesus. I wondered if you were a Christian when I heard your comment about the Lord providing. Isn't it just like the Lord to lead us to you?" Mrs. Hayden nodded as Dad continued: "What's the back-yard like?"

"There are twigs down all over—no big branches, though," Mrs. Hayden answered.

"Here's our plan: Max, Mitch, and I will work in front, while the girls and Mom start out back."

"I'll help the ladies." Mrs. Hayden seemed happy. "Do you have to plug in the chainsaw?"

Dad smiled as he glanced at the orange piece of equipment. It was old, but Mr. Delome had kept it well maintained. "No, it runs on gas. Do you have a way to burn wood in your house, like maybe a fireplace?"

"Yes. I have a wood-burning stove in the basement."

"Good." Dad carried the chainsaw, gas can, safety glasses, gloves, and ear protectors to the grass and set them down. "The wood from the tree will be great firewood after it dries out a bit."

"What a perfect idea!" exclaimed Mrs. Hayden. "We have a wood bin behind our house where you could put most of it. I don't know what we'll do with all of the large sticks though."

"We brought twine to bundle them. The small twigs can be discarded in trash bags."

Max and Mitch grabbed the supplies the girls would need, and everyone but Dad followed Mrs. Hayden to the back-

"Good." Dad carried the chainsaw, gas can, safety glasses, gloves, and ear protectors to the grass and set them down.

yard. She unlatched the wooden gate, and it creaked open. "My neighbor's dog likes to chase squirrels in my yard if he can manage to squeeze in. I try to keep the gate latched, otherwise he'll bump the gate with his nose, and then he's in the yard! Today it's fine to leave open, because those neighbors are on vacation."

Mrs. Hayden's yard was slightly sloped, and several trees afforded a welcome amount of shade. Yellow-and-white striped patio furniture was set inside a screened-in back porch. Mollie noticed a large amount of small twigs scattered across the green lawn. The boys set the supplies down and went to help Dad.

"Let's get busy," Mom said with a spark of energy. Mollie and Maddie took a few trash bags and went to the north end of the yard while Mrs. Hayden and Mom started on the area next to the porch. Mom parked the stroller in the shade of a nearby oak tree and locked the wheels.

"They're sure cute," Mrs. Hayden commented. "How old are they?"

"Three months tomorrow." Mom and Mrs. Hayden continued to chat as they worked, with Mom peeking at the twins frequently.

Meanwhile, Mollie and Maddie found many things to talk about. "We need to decide what we're giving Dad for Father's Day," Mollie told Maddie.

"What is Father's Day?" Maddie plucked a green leaf from a stick and poked the leaf at something on the branch. "Look, Mollie! Here's a cateriller."

"A what?"

"A cateriller!"

Mollie bent over to look at what Maddie's leaf was touching. The insect's green body moved with a flowing action. "Oh, it's a caterpillar! Mitch would like him."

"May I give it to Mitch?"

"Not now. If you leave the branch there on the brick, we'll tell him about it next time we see him."

"But Mollie, I really want to know about Father's Day."

"It's like Mother's Day, but this is a day set aside to honor dads. We do extra nice things for our dad and give him a present. Maddie, you may put the big sticks in a pile; we'll tie them up later. Only the tiny ones go in the bag."

"I am nice to Daddy lots of times," Maddie decided. "But," she said after a pause, "I don't give him a present every day."

"We bought Mom a pretty apron for Mother's Day," Mollie remembered. "Grandma helped us find the perfect one. Maybe she would have ideas for Dad."

After a while, Mollie realized Mom was working by herself. "Mrs. Hayden must have gone inside," Mollie remarked. "Maddie, come on! We'll help Mom."

Mom's face lit up as the girls joined her. "Now I won't have to be lonely; Mrs. Hayden went to get drinks for everyone, and the twins seem happy enough for the moment," Mom explained.

Fifteen minutes later, Mrs. Hayden bustled out with a tray. "Sorry it took me so long: I'm fussy about getting my lemonade to the perfect strength!" The screen door slammed behind her. Mrs. Hayden handed each one a cup. "Mollie and Madelyn, would you take the tray out front and give your brothers and dad some?"

"Yes, ma'am," Mollie agreed, taking the tray.

Maddie looked in her cup. "It's pink lemonade," she announced, and then she whispered to Mollie as they walked away, "She called me Madelyn!"

Mrs. Hayden turned to Mom. "I thought of two things while I was inside mixing up the lemonade. I have a friend who lives on Strawberry Lane! Would you happen to know a Maud Bagwell?"

"We do," Mom responded. "Mrs. Bagwell lives a few houses from us."

"What a small world! I've known her for years, although I hardly see her—about the only place we bump into each other is at the grocery store. The other question is where do you all worship on Sundays?"

"We are a part of a church that is a little ways out in the country, but starting this Sunday, our church is beginning a ministry at Delaware Heights Nursing Home. We're leading that outreach along with a few others from our church. We will have a morning worship service every Sunday in the nursing home."

"My husband is recovering from a broken hip at Delaware Heights!" Mrs. Hayden exclaimed.

"Because I hadn't seen your husband, I thought you must be a widow," Mom said. "I didn't think about the possibility of your husband being in the nursing home!" Mom turned to the stroller as a loud cry rose from it. "Excuse me."

The girls came back with several fewer cups on the tray. "Mitch took two," Maddie informed.

Mrs. Hayden had a twinkle in her eyes. "Good! I had done a few extra in case anyone was really thirsty."

Mom picked up Melissa, who was crying. "I think Miss Melissa needs to be in the sling, but I left it in the van."

Moses joined the crying session, and Maddie peeked at him. "Uh oh, Mommy, now Moses is unhappy!"

"That's how it works sometimes." Mom spoke a little louder over their cries. "Mollie, you may hold Moses on the patio; there's a chair you can sit in. Both babies are tired, so I'm hoping they'll go to sleep soon. They have been very good watching us work. It may be that we don't get much done for the moment."

Out front, Dad and the boys were making steady progress. Standing by the portion of the tree that touched the ground, Dad gripped the orange chainsaw firmly with gloved hands, concentrating on the contact his chainsaw made with the wood. A large chunk plunged into the grass as the chainsaw sliced through the wood. Mitch gathered twigs a safe distance away, dropping them in a pile on the driveway, while Max cut up the large sticks with the hand clippers. Dad stopped the chainsaw and pulled his red ear protectors off.

"Is something wrong?" Max asked.

"No, I just needed a little break." Dad removed his safety glasses and wiped sweat from his eyes. "As the saying goes, wood warms you twice: once when you're cutting it, and once when you're burning it! Where's the lemonade you saved?"

Max ran to the steps to retrieve the cup for Dad. "Thanks." Dad gratefully drained the entire cup.

"Would you see how we're doing?" Mitch asked.

Dad checked on the boys' progress. "Looks good to me. Max, you might try cutting the sticks a little smaller; it'll make them easier to bundle."

Just then, Mom carried Melissa around front. "Would you please unlock the van for me?" Mom asked.

"Sure." Fishing the keys from his pocket, Dad pushed the unlock button on the black keyless-entry device. "How are the twins faring?"

"It's supposed to be their nap time, so they're a little fussy. I thought I'd put Melissa in the sling. Mollie's holding Moses."

After Mom left, Dad pulled on the chainsaw cord, but the motor sputtered. He yanked several more times, and finally the chainsaw came to life. Mitch shouted to Max, "I really like being a part of I-J-N! I wish it would storm more often!"

Chapter 4

The Surprise "Visitor"

In the backyard, progress was slow. Mrs. Hayden was inside on the phone, Mollie held Moses, and Mom was settling Melissa in the sling. Maddie hurried around picking up twigs. "See, Mommy," she called. "I'm a big girl—I'm working all by myself!"

"You're being very diligent. Mollie is going to help now, too, since Moses fell asleep." Before putting the sleeping baby in the stroller, Mom laid the seat back so Moses would be more comfortable. "Mollie, thanks for taking care of him," Mom said as she patted her shoulder. "You are doing very well with the twins, and I'm grateful for the help!"

"You're welcome." Mollie went over to Maddie and told her, "This area is pretty well cleaned up; let's go over near the fence." The girls strolled to the new section and began working several feet from each other. Maddie chattered about being happy that Grandpa and Grandma were moving next door.

At that moment, Max and Mitch showed up. "Hi!" Mitch said. "We're thirsty again. Where's the lemonade?"

"Mrs. Hayden left the tray on the table near Mom," Mollie answered. "Maddie saved something to show you over there on that brick."

The boys stopped, turning to look where Mollie was pointing. Mitch immediately picked up the squirmy caterpillar. "Thanks, Maddie. He's a pretty neat little guy."

"MOLLIE!" Maddie cried, and Mollie whirled around to see Maddie standing perfectly still.

The urgency in Maddie's voice caused both boys to rush over to them. "What's wrong?" Mitch blurted. Almost exactly half way between the girls, partially hidden among the grass, was a black snake with a yellow stripe down its body. It hadn't seen Mollie, but its beady eyes were focused on Maddie and the boys.

Max observed the snake's color and head shape. "It's just a garter, Maddie."

"No, Max, it's a snake!" Maddie didn't seem to be impressed with Max's knowledge of reptiles.

"A garter is a type of snake; it's not poisonous," Max assured her. "He eats insects and stuff; garters are good for yards." As he spoke, the snake turned and quickly slithered underneath the fence.

"There he goes!" Mitch yelled excitedly, hurrying over to the fence. "Yes, I see him headed for some bushes in the next yard!"

Noticing all the commotion, Mrs. Hayden stepped out on her back porch and asked, "What happened?"

It hadn't seen Mollie, but its beady eyes
were focused on Maddie and the boys.

"Maddie found a garter snake," Mom said matter-of-factly.

"A snake?" Mrs. Hayden repeated. "Why I've never seen one in my yard before!"

"He was a very, very bad snake!" Maddie sniffled. "I didn't like him."

"I'm trying to locate my two workers," Dad joined the group in the backyard. "Did I hear Maddie mention a snake?"

"Yes! He was near me," Maddie said, "but he ran off."

"It was only a garter snake, and he wasn't big," Mitch explained. "I'm glad Max and I had come for more lemonade—which we still need—because the girls were frightened. The snake is gone, though." Mitch, who had still been holding the caterpillar, carefully released him on a low tree branch.

"I don't want to work here anymore," Maddie decided, dropping a handful of twigs.

"You'll be fine, Maddie," Dad reassured her. "He was more scared of you than you were of him. He shouldn't come back while you're working. I'll tell you, Maddie, I don't like snakes either. After all, the Lord cursed them in Genesis. At least you children didn't pet-sit snakes last summer!"

Maddie wiped her tears. "Okay, Daddy." She patted Mom's sling. "Mommy, may I please kiss Melissa?"

"Sure." Mom bent down so Maddie could reach the baby.

"Her eyes are closed, Mommy."

"I know; I'm happy she's asleep."

"Anyone hungry?" Mrs. Hayden asked, looking around at the children. "I'll fix lunch now."

"We are, but is there something we can do to help?" Mom wondered.

"No, I can manage; I have a plan."

"Grandpa called a little earlier," Dad told the family as he dusted wood chips off his shirt. "He wondered what we were doing today. He said that the city will be picking up sticks if they're bundled. That'd be perfect for us: we'll put our bundles by the curb this afternoon as we finish. His purpose for the call, though, was to tell me he's dropping by church after work to pick up hymn books for the nursing home on Sunday."

After lunch, the whole family climbed into the van so Dad could take Mom and the twins home. Dad helped Mom carry the twins upstairs, and the family set off again, minus three of their group. By mid-afternoon, bundles of sticks were neatly piled along a strip of grass near the street. A nice pile of trash bags sat next to them. The wood from the tree had been stacked in the backyard for the Haydens' future use in their wood stove, and everything looked tidy. Mrs. Hayden's eyes sparkled. "I can't thank you enough. I knew we'd have to pay someone for the tree removal, and you'll offend me if you won't take this." Mrs. Hayden handed two twenty-dollar bills to Dad. "It's not much, but I intend for you to have it."

Dad shook his head. "We only wanted to help you."

"Yes, I know, but this is my way of thanking you. Would you please take it? Maybe you could have a family pizza party with it or give it away." Mrs. Hayden thrust the money into Dad's hand. "Oh, what time is the service Sunday?"

"Nine-thirty," replied Dad. "If you insist, we'll take the money, but we certainly didn't expect it or do it for that reason. We'll look forward to seeing you and meeting your husband on Sunday!"

On the way home, Dad turned down Grandma Clifton's street. "I meant to check on her yard before we started." They drove to the small house, where Grandma Clifton was on her porch, with Honey sitting next to her. Dad pulled into the driveway and rolled down his window. "Hello!"

"It's good to see you," Grandma Clifton greeted them, while Honey jumped to her feet, wagging her tail.

"We wanted to check on your yard. It looks like things are fine."

"They are. I only had a few sticks down, and I took care of them this morning." Grandma Clifton tucked a silver strand of hair behind her ear. "It was good exercise for me."

"I'm sorry we didn't check on you earlier," Dad apologized.

"Don't feel badly. I really would call you if I had a need," Grandma Clifton reassured him. "I'm grateful for the Lord's protection during the storm."

Dad waved, and they drove home. "I'm tired," Mitch declared, "but it's a good tired. I wouldn't trade anything for helping Mrs. Hayden. She seemed really happy we helped her, and I think she enjoyed our company."

Max agreed. "I like to do projects and help people. What are you going to do with the money she gave us?"

Dad pushed the button to open the garage door. "I wonder what you all would think if we gave it to our national pastor's family." The Moodys supported a native pastor in Africa and occasionally sent him a letter. They also received regular reports from him.

"Perfect!" Max exclaimed. "We worked in Jesus' Name, and now we can send the money we were given to our pastor in Jesus' Name. I-J-N keeps on serving the Lord. Maybe the Lord will give us more I-J-N projects."

At dinner, Mom asked Mollie, "When were you going to plant those sunflower seeds Grandma gave us?"

"I have been meaning to, but then I forget. Is it too late to plant them?"

"Hmmm." Mom consulted the calendar. "It should still be okay, although it is much later than we usually plant. Jim, do you think after we're through eating, the girls could plant the seeds, and the boys could clean up before family Bible time?"

"That's fine."

"Dad," Mitch protested, looking at the number of dishes that would need to be washed. "Can't the girls wait until they help with cleanup? It'll take Max and me forever!"

"No, they need to get the planting done. Mitch, do you remember what the Lord thought of the Israelites complaining?" Mitch paused and then shook his head. "It says in Numbers," Dad explained, "that the Lord was displeased with them, and He gave them consequences for their complaining. Philippians 2:14 says, 'Do all things without murmurings and disputing.' Complaining, which is what you were doing, is a serious thing, Son."

"Yes, sir."

The girls went to the garage where Mollie located two small hand shovels and a little rake. She gave Maddie the envelope with seeds, and they walked to the backyard. "Mom said we could plant them over there." Mollie pointed to a section near the fence. "They're supposed to grow eight feet tall." Kneeling on the mulch, Mollie used the rake to scrape back the layer of wood chips.

"Mollie, look! A worm!" The dirt was soggy from the rain, and Maddie used the small shovel to pick up an exposed wiggling earthworm. "I don't like him, but he's not as bad as a snake." Soon, the sunflowers were planted and watered, and the Moodys gathered in the living room for family Bible time.

Chapter 5

A New Experience

Sunday morning dawned, bringing with it a day much anticipated by the Moodys. It was their first Sunday of having a church service at the nursing home. The night before, Max had asked Mom if he and Mitch could start making Sunday breakfast for the family. Max and Mitch were in the kitchen promptly at 7:15 to start preparations for an eight o'clock breakfast. Mitch glanced at the open cookbook. "Just tell me what to do, Max."

Max read through the recipe. "You can grab the oatmeal from the pantry, and I'll find the other ingredients."

In a half hour, the inviting smell of pancakes wafted through the house. Dad walked into the kitchen with Moses. "Good morning, boys."

"Hi!" Max responded, flipping a pancake.

"I hope they're as good as they look," Dad commented.

"I've already tried one," Mitch confessed. "They ARE great!"

Mom joined them in the kitchen. "Good morning; it smells delicious." Melissa was in the sling, and she let out a happy coo. Mom turned to Dad. "I've been thinking about church and how that affects the twins' nap. If we bring the stroller with us, the twins would have a better possibility of sleeping, and it would also be easier than you and me holding them the whole service."

"It's worth a try."

"Would you please bring Moses upstairs so I can get him dressed for church?" Mom asked.

"Sure," Dad agreed.

Maddie clambered halfway down the stairs, stopping to try to tie the bow on her dress. "What are you doing?" Mom asked when she saw Maddie.

"Trying to tie my bow." Maddie strained to see her bow.

"I have Melissa so I can't help, but I'm sure someone else will. Doing that on the stairs isn't the safest place. I'd like you to pick up the twins' toys in the living room because we're having guests for lunch. I didn't get that done last night."

"Yes, ma'am." Maddie skipped into the living room to take care of the toys. A few minutes later, Maddie wandered into the kitchen. "Hi, boys! Do you like my bow?"

Mitch grabbed a gallon of milk from the refrigerator and said, "It's crooked; I'll re-tie it for you."

"I did it all by myself." Maddie turned to Max: "How does my bow look?"

"It is probably okay," he mumbled, hurrying to put the Mexican refried beans into a pot.

"Why are you doin' that?" Maddie wondered.

"The beans are for burritos at lunch; Mom wanted me to put them in the oven so they can heat up while we're at church."

"Oh. Max, you still haven't looked at my bow," Maddie reminded him.

"I'm busy."

"Please."

Max reluctantly turned his attention to Maddie. "It's pretty lopsided. Mollie would be a good one to help; I'm going to call everyone for breakfast."

Maddie sighed. "Mollie is getting ready for church. Mitch said he would re-tie it, but I don't think he would do it right." Maddie shook her head solemnly as she hurried to the table and scooted onto her chair.

After Mom finished her last pancake, she said: "I'm excusing myself to feed the twins. Breakfast was delicious; they tasted better than my pancakes!"

By 8:45, the kitchen was spotless. "Ten-minute warning!" Dad called from his room. The children hurried to brush their teeth and do last-minute preparations.

As Dad buckled Moses into his car seat, Mollie giggled. "You're cute, Moses. Mom dressed you all up." She tugged at his small overall straps, and Moses rewarded her with a smile.

Pastor Thompson had given his whole-hearted approval and support to the new ministry. He had hand-picked Jason and Kate Parker to help them. Jason and Kate were a young couple who had hearts to serve the Lord Jesus. Although they hadn't been able to have children yet, they kept busy ministering in different areas. Pastor Thompson had also agreed that Grandpa and Grandma would be a great asset to the ministry, and they were anxiously awaiting the first Sunday.

On the short drive over, Dad gave instructions to the family: "I always want you children staying near or with an adult. Here's the plan. Grandpa will go with Max and Mitch to invite people to come to church, while Grandma and Mollie will be another inviting team. By the way, when you go to someone's room, it's really like their bedroom, and they might not be expecting guests. So, it's important to knock first before going in. Say something like, 'Good morning. May I come in?' Mr. Parker, Mrs. Parker, and Maddie will set up the dining room and visit with the elderly who are waiting for the service. Mom will also stay in the dining room with the twins and chat with the residents. I plan to be out inviting people to attend as well as helping Mr. Parker with setup if he needs it." Even though Dad and Mom didn't call Mr. and Mrs. Parker by their last name, in conversation they referred to them in that way so as not to confuse the children. The children addressed adults by their last name as a matter of respect.

When they arrived at the nursing home, Mitch noticed a large wet spot on the front of Melissa's outfit. "Mom! Melissa spit up—on her Sunday dress!"

Mom sighed. "Grab a wash cloth from the diaper bag; it's probably in the outer pocket."

"May I take off my seatbelt?" Mitch asked.

"Let me park first; then you may," Dad said, finding a place to pull the van into.

Mitch waited for Dad and then unbuckled his seatbelt and struggled for the diaper bag. "It's not easy to reach." His voice sounded muffled as he stretched for the elusive item. "Got it!" He pulled out the wash cloth and dabbed at Melissa's dress. "She's still pretty damp."

"Hopefully she'll dry," Mom said.

Mitch felt the dress. "Maybe, but she's sure not going to smell very good."

"Oh, well," Mom remarked as they unloaded from the van. "It'll have to be the way it is. Next week I will try to remember to put a change of clothes in the diaper bag for each baby. I'm just going to be grateful it was only Melissa and not Moses too."

Maddie climbed out behind Max. "You know, Maddie," Max turned to her. "The Lord convicted me that I was preoccupied earlier when you wanted me to look at your bow. Please forgive me for not paying attention to you."

"I forgive you."

Grandpa and Grandma pulled in beside the Moodys. "Good morning," Grandpa said. "Isn't this a beautiful day the Lord Jesus gave us?"

"It is," Dad agreed.

Max set up the stroller so Dad and Mom could put the twins in it. "Thanks, Max." Mom squeezed his shoulder.

Grandma bent down to give each of the twins a kiss. "Melissa has a bit of spit up on her chin, and the front of her dress feels a little wet, Emily," Grandma informed her.

"You're right," Mitch said. "I noticed she spit up as we arrived! I guess I missed cleaning up her chin."

Grandpa chuckled. "Life with babies."

A four-door white car entered the lot and parked next to the van. "Hi, Jason," Grandpa greeted the man who jumped out. Mr. Parker was in his early thirties, and he was of an average height with dark hair, blue eyes, and a square jaw.

"Hi, Mr. Moody!" Mr. Parker opened the door for his wife. Her brown shoulder-length hair bobbed as an irresistible smile lit up her face.

"It's so wonderful to see you," Mrs. Parker said as she gave Mom a hug. "Jason and I've been looking forward to this all week."

Mr. Parker reached inside his car to pop the trunk latch. "I borrowed a podium from church." He lifted out a cherry-color podium. "Pastor Thompson said we were welcome to it; they're not using it right now," Mr. Parker explained to Grandpa and Dad. "I also have the small sound system, but I brought a hand cart to help us get it in." He opened the back car door, grabbed the cart, stacked two speakers on it, and then put a plastic container on top.

"Do you need help?" Grandpa asked.

"You can get the podium; I'll truck in the other stuff." The group walked toward the entrance to Delaware Heights, with Max and Mitch hurrying ahead.

Mitch held open the first set of glass doors while Max went to the next set. He pushed the button that unlocked the double doors, and he held it open as everyone entered.

A thin, older lady sat in a chair next to the door with her legs crossed, and she wore a bright purple vinyl bracelet around her wrist. Seeing the Moodys, she stood up. "Hi," she said, moving toward the door. *Reeeeeeerrrrororo, reeeeeeerrrrororo.* The siren seemed to pierce the air, and the twins began crying. Mom pushed the stroller away from the blaring noise. The older lady shrugged and plopped herself back in the chair.

A nurse ran for the keypad next to the door and punched in several numbers, which made the siren abruptly stop. "Do you want me to move?" offered the older lady, her legs crossed again, and one foot jiggling up and down.

"That'd be great, Henrietta."

"I'm so sorry," said a lady as she approached the group. She looked familiar, and Mitch saw *Jennifer* in clear letters on her name tag. *That's right, she's the activities director,* he thought. Jennifer explained in a low voice, "We have several residents who like to wander, and they wear an arm band that sets the alarm off if they get too close to the door. We had to start using the bands because one resident was found on the main road! Henrietta likes to sit there, and she's been setting off the alarm. I'm sorry the alarm made the babies cry, although I am glad you brought them! They sure are cute, and it looks like they have settled down already."

"They are just entering that stage of being a little interested in what's going on around them," Dad responded. "The alarm didn't trouble them for long."

Grandpa and the boys took off down the first hallway. They walked past the nurses' station where several residents sat sleeping in their wheelchairs. "We'll see about inviting them later," Grandpa decided. "Let's go down this hall." An elderly man was slowly wheeling himself along, gripping the railing with one hand and using the other to propel the wheelchair. They caught up to him, and Grandpa said, "Good morning."

A pleasant smile crossed the man's wrinkled face, while he ran his fingers through a receding silvery hairline. "Hi."

"We're going to have a church service in your dining room. Would you like to come?"

The man played with a button on his black leather vest. "What kind of service?"

"It's Christian." Grandpa stood near the man.

"I'm not of that religion."

Max glanced at Grandpa who nodded. "We're happy for anyone to come; we preach from the Bible," Max encouraged him.

"Well, I might check it out. Did you say it's in the dining room?"

"Yes, sir!"

The three continued to an open door where they could see a man was watching TV. Max knocked on the door. "Good morning! May we come in?" Max asked.

"What do you want?" a gruff voice called.

"We'd like to invite you to come to church—"

"Not interested," the man interrupted, keeping his eyes fixed on the TV.

"Okay—maybe next week," Mitch suggested hopefully as they left. Walking to another room, Mitch read the name plaque near the door. "Harold Hayden. Oh! We know his wife."

A tall man with a walker stood in front of a small mirror, combing his white hair. Before Max could say anything, he turned toward Grandpa and the boys. "Good morning," he said.

"Mr. Hayden," Max grinned. "I'm Max Moody, and our family helped Mrs. Hayden clean up your yard the other day."

Mr. Hayden set the comb on the dresser, grasped his walker, and moved slowly toward them. He firmly shook each of their hands. "Lucille can't stop talking about your family; I'm grateful for all the help you offered. If it wasn't for this bad hip, I would have been out doing it myself."

"We enjoyed our project, and we even came across a snake!" Mitch told him.

"That's not a surprise. I find them all the time, but," Mr. Hayden lowered his voice, "I never tell Lucille because she'd get all upset."

"Would you like to come to church in the dining room?"

"Sure. Lucille told me you're having a service; I'll come with her when she gets here, which should be any time."

The boys and Grandpa met Grandma and Mollie. "Any success?" Mollie wondered.

"Yes!"

"Good." Grandma was pleased. "Mollie and I've had several who say they are coming and two more we have pushed down to the dining room in their wheelchairs." Grandma knocked on an open door across the hall.

A tall woman with curly gray hair sat in a rocking chair. "Come in! You two look delightful!" she exclaimed.

Mollie went over to the lady. "My name is Mollie."

"Nice to meet you; I'm Hazel Dunlap."

"Would you like to come to church this morning? It's being held in the dining room."

"I would like that."

"We'll give you a push down." As Mollie and Grandma took her to the dining room, they met Dad, also bringing someone to church.

Jennifer nodded at Mollie as they reached the dining room at the same time. "You'll love Mrs. Dunlap," she said, patting Mollie's arm. "Let's see. Who else do we still need?"

A few ladies gathered around Mom. "Are they twins?" one lady asked, pointing to the stroller.

"Yes, they are. This one is Moses, and this one is Melissa."

"They're really cute."

Mr. and Mrs. Parker had scooted the dining room tables to the edge of the room and set up chairs in two rows. As the elderly people came in, Mr. Parker directed where the wheelchairs would go, making a few neat rows. Several appeared to have hearing problems, so he placed them near a speaker. The speakers were laid on tables on each side of the portion of the dining room they used for church. Maddie's job was to distribute the hymn books, and she cheerfully gave each person a book. One aide in navy scrubs rolled in a tiny lady. Turning to Mollie, she said, "This is Myrnice LaFerre."

Mrs. LaFerre had short gray speckled hair and eyes that sparkled with life. She gave Mollie a hug. "I'm so glad you're going to have church this morning. I did have a little

As the elderly people came in, Mr. Parker directed where the wheelchairs would go, making a few neat rows.

problem, but I've figured out a plan. I'm often sleepy in the mornings since I have to take a pain pill." Mrs. LaFerre glanced over to make sure the aide was gone. "See?" She opened her hand. "I'm saving it for after church."

It was only a minute until the clock read nine-thirty, so the children hurried to find a place to sit. Dad grabbed the microphone off the table and switched it on. "We're so glad to have you all here," he addressed the group. "It's a beautiful morning—another day the Lord Jesus has given us. I want to introduce everyone. We're the Moodys, and my wife Emily is in the back with our twins, Moses and Melissa. Just so you know, because of illnesses that can be spread at care homes, we won't be passing the twins around. Since babies have a propensity to stick their hands in their mouths, we would be grateful if you don't hold their hands. My oldest is Max—why don't you children stand up when I call your name?—then we have Mollie, and then Mitch. My next-to-youngest daughter is Maddie. We're thrilled to have four others joining us: my parents, James and Martha Moody, and another couple, Jason and Kate Parker. Jason is going to lead us in our time of singing."

Mr. Parker grasped the microphone. "Good morning. We'll be a little untraditional, because we want you all to pick out what songs we'll sing. Each of you should have a book, and if you don't, raise your hand and we'll get you one."

Mrs. Parker sat on the piano bench, waiting for the first song to be chosen. It didn't take long before "113" was called out. "113," Mr. Parker repeated. "The Old Rugged Cross." Mitch noticed that several people seemed to be looking for the page but not finding it, so he and Max began assisting those who needed help.

Grandma picked the next song, while the boys jumped to the task of page-finding. "Young man," a lady's voice called from the back. "Please help me find the number." Mitch worked his way to her row and carefully stepped down it. He had almost reached her, when he stumbled over her neighbor's foot.

"OUCH!" the lady glowered darkly at him.

"I'm sorry, Ma'am."

She shook her head with a sour expression. "You'd better be."

Mitch walked around her and helped the lady who had requested it. When he was through, he turned to leave, deciding to go out the opposite way. Mrs. LaFerre tapped him. "Don't mind her," she whispered. "She's just a grouch; you didn't hurt her, only caught her by surprise. She complains all the time to the aides." Mitch was grateful for the assurance because he felt badly for hurting the lady.

Grandpa stepped up to the little pulpit, taking the microphone Mr. Parker held out to him. "We're going to take prayer requests. This is an open time, so feel free to share."

Grandpa pulled a small notebook from his pocket. "Today is five twenty-nine."

"What was that number?" a familiar voice in the back called out.

"I was just writing down the date, May 29th. We will have another hymn after prayer if there is time," Grandpa tried to keep a straight face. "Does anyone have a prayer request?"

Mom stood behind the last row of wheelchairs, pushing the stroller back and forth, at a steady pace, in hopes the twins would fall asleep. She peeked at them and saw Moses' eyes looking heavy, but Melissa was wide awake and grinned at Mom.

A lady raised her hand. "I have one. I've not been feeling well for several weeks, so the doctors are running tests. Please pray that they will find the cause of my discomfort."

"Yes, we certainly will."

Mrs. LaFerre spoke: "I would like prayer for patience. There are always many needs here and not enough workers to come as quickly as one would like. I desire to patiently wait for help."

"Yes, patience is something all of us can use."

After Grandpa prayed for the requests, Dad took Grandpa's place. "It has been a joy to prepare a message for our service this morning. Let's open with a word of prayer." Mom glanced at the twins who were now fast asleep. She scooted a chair over so she could sit next to them during Dad's message.

When the service was over, Dad and Max talked to an elderly gentleman named LeRoy McGovern. "I have to tell you," the dark-skinned man said as he adjusted himself in his wheelchair, "I was a pastor for sixty years, and I'm not lying!" Mr. McGovern's eyes gleamed with the joy of the Lord, and he rubbed his white speckled goatee. "I like this home alright, but they had no worship service on Sunday morning! I've been praying and fasting for a man of God to come. Sundays used to be my going-to-meeting day; what a day of rejoicing that was. My heart has been singing the entire service over your family being here; not many people will come to a nursing home to have a church service on Sunday morning."

Dad smiled as his hand seemed to disappear in the man's firm grasp. "It's our joy!"

Grandma chatted with Mrs. LaFerre. "How long have you lived here?" Grandma asked.

"About five years. My husband died, and then I fell and broke my leg. I originally came to recover, but it seemed lonely at home with Henry being gone, so I decided to stay."

"I'm sorry to hear about your husband. Do you have family nearby?"

Mrs. LaFerre nodded. "My son and daughter-in-law live ten minutes away. They come once or twice a week to visit. Where do you live?"

"We live about ten minutes away too," Grandma replied. "Our son and his family live a block from here. We recently bought the house next door to them, so we plan to move later this summer."

"Really?" Mrs. LaFerre pulled a tissue from where she kept it under the wristband of her watch. "Your grandkids are awfully sweet. We don't see a lot of children here, so it's a treat when people bring them."

Mollie asked Mrs. LaFerre if she was ready to go back to her room. "I guess so. I think I'll need to stop and ask a nurse for a drink of water." Her eyes twinkled at Mollie. "Remember?"

"I remember, but I hope you're not hurting." Mollie tried not to worry.

"I'm fine."

Mollie stopped next to a nurse's medicine cart. "Excuse me, could we please have a cup of water for Mrs. LaFerre?"

The nurse handed them a paper cup with water in it. "Here you go." Mrs. LaFerre held on to the cup, and Mollie pushed her back to her room, with Grandma following.

Around eleven, the men loaded the sound equipment into Mr. Parker's car, and everyone piled into their vehicles to make the short drive to the Moodys' house. On the way home, Mollie told the story about Mrs. LaFerre. "There was this one lady who wanted to come to church, and she decided not to take her pain pill so she could stay awake. I was nervous she would be in lots of pain, but she said she was fine."

"What did she look like?" Mitch was trying to picture who Mrs. LaFerre was.

"She had short gray hair, and she was in a wheelchair," Mollie said.

"Mollie," Max protested, "you are describing almost every lady there! You have to be more specific!"

Dad chuckled as he listened to their conversation. When they pulled into the driveway, the twins were wide awake. Mom glanced at the clock. "They should still be napping, but I don't think they will sleep anymore."

"I know who would love to take care of them," Dad said, unbuckling Moses from his seat and nodding as Mr. and Mrs. Parker walked in through the open garage door. Dad smiled and told them, "Emily said they're not going to nap, so if you'd like, you're welcome to hold them while lunch is being prepared."

"We'd love to," Mr. Parker answered. "But we'll wash up first." After a delightful dinner, their guests stayed to fellowship with the Moodys until two o'clock.

That night, as Mollie and Maddie were going to sleep, Mollie had an idea. "Maddie, I saw how Mrs. Parker really liked holding Moses and Melissa. Mrs. Parker said that she would love to have her own babies, but the Lord hasn't given her any yet. We should start praying every night that the Lord would give her a baby. Isn't that a good plan?"

"Yes," Maddie responded. "Babies are nice, and maybe Mommy would let us share our babies with her sometimes." Maddie paused thoughtfully. "I could even let her hold my doll, Abigail."

Chapter 6

The In-House Move

Memorial Day was here, and the Moodys had invited Grandpa, Grandma, and Grandma Clifton over for a barbecue that evening. It was also Grandma's birthday, so they would be celebrating with a special dessert and a few gifts.

Mom pulled an egg, sausage, and cheese breakfast casserole from the oven and tested it. "It's not quite done."

"I'm very hungry," Mitch commented, peering around Mom at the casserole.

"You won't have to wait much longer," Mom assured him.

Dad dumped a can of frozen orange juice concentrate and another of cranberry concentrate into a large pitcher. He then filled up the container with the designated number of cans of water. "I'm glad we get Rosie's juice with breakfast," Mitch observed.

"Mom thought it would be a nice treat; I was going to mix it up last night, but I forgot. I'll just stick some ice cubes in to help it get cold."

"Where did we get that name Rosie's juice?" Mitch asked.

"As the story goes, Grandpa and Grandma were on a trip to California several years ago, and at one hotel, they had this juice. They asked the breakfast hostess what kind of juice it was; she told them it was called Rosie's juice. She explained the juice was her own simple creation: an equal mixture of orange juice and cranberry juice. Hotel guests nicknamed the juice after her."

Soon, the family was settled around the table. "Let's pray," Dad said as he rearranged Moses to his other arm. "Dear Heavenly Father, what a gracious God we serve. Your mercies are truly new every morning. Please bless this food, and watch over our day. In Jesus' Name, Amen."

Mom served the casserole while Mollie poured the juice. "We have some things to share with you," Dad announced. "I guess you know there are only two more days of school left, and then Thursday and Friday you'll do testing at Grandma's house."

Several heads nodded. "First, I want to talk about chores. Mom needs to be doing less of the household work since the twins take a lot more of her time than one baby would. Mom feels she's not been very organized in the chore department, especially with checking chores and even assigning them. She recently worked through a book on chores and how to do a chore system. Here." Dad reached for a book he had set on the floor before breakfast. "I'll try to explain it. The picture shows a little plastic pack having a clip at the top filled with chore cards. From what Mom tells me, you'll clip the pack onto your clothes and then do what the chore cards tell you to do. Emily, when do they wear the packs?"

Mom's face lit up, and they could tell she was excited. "They'll put them on before their morning Bible time."

Mom jumped up and grabbed the children's ChorePacks. "Let me see what Mollie's pack contains," Dad said, taking the top pack off the stack. "The first card says Read Bible/Pray. You know about that one." He flipped another card. "Put Nightgown Away. You can do that, right?" Mollie giggled. "Good, I thought so. Make Bed. That should be simple. Pick Up Room. Hmmm ... would my girls leave things out?" Maddie shrugged her shoulders. "I won't go through them all, but you get the idea. Each of you has a few new chores to help relieve Mom's load."

"What 'bout mine, Daddy? I can't read that."

"I don't know," Dad agreed.

"You have your own special one with pictures," Mom smiled, handing Maddie's over.

"May I look at mine?" Mitch requested.

"Sure." Mom gave Max and Mitch their packs while Dad passed Mollie hers.

Mitch flipped through his cards. "I'm going to like this. I always get distracted and forget what I'm supposed to be doing. This should be the end of lunch cleanups I get when I don't finish my chores. Watch it," Mitch pointed to Maddie's left hand. "You have something on you."

"It's just little bits dirty," Maddie remarked, wiping the red gooey substance on her jumper. "All gone."

"Maddie! That was ketchup, and it'll stain your jumper." Mitch shook his head. "Your napkin is supposed to be used for wiping your hands, not your dress."

"No one gave me one," Maddie protested. "Mommy washes my jumpers, so it'll be okay."

"It looks like I have yours!" Mitch offered his extra napkin to Maddie. Maddie licked it to dampen the napkin and then rubbed at her jumper, trying to make the ketchup stain go away, but it only became worse. She turned her attention back to her ChorePack. "May I do this thing today?"

"If you want to," Mom agreed. "I wasn't going to use them until next week."

"Emily, why don't you share about our special event this summer?"

"We're going to have an Independence Day breakfast picnic for our neighbors!"

"That's the best news of all!" Mitch mumbled, his mouth stuffed full of casserole. After a warning glance from Dad, he closed his mouth, rapidly chewed, and then swallowed. "Do you think we could invite Grandpa and Grandma?"

"Yes, we'll invite them." Dad pushed back his plate. "The casserole was delicious; thanks, Emily. We're going to have the picnic in the morning, because it'll be cooler, and some people have plans for events later in the day. Mom and you all will plan the details a little later. Now, for a change of subject. Max came to me a week ago to ask me to pray about a Moody children business this summer, but he wasn't sure what it would be. Pet-sitting is not an option, because we don't want to have strange animals in the house with the twins being little. Maple is a great pet, but one is enough." Dad fondly glanced at the golden retriever who was curled up in the corner. "Grandpa asked if you boys could help him do projects on his house next door two afternoons a week, and Grandma would like Mollie to help her clean to prepare the house for moving in. They want to pay you for your work, and you want to have a summer business. It seemed like a perfect match. We gave them our permission."

"That'll be exciting!" Mitch declared.

"This stuff is not coming off." Maddie had dipped the napkin into a glass of water and then rubbed at the spot on her jumper. "I've seen Mitch clean his pants with napkin water when he spills on himself. I really want to wear this for Grandma's birthday."

Mom smiled at her. "I have a bit of laundry to do, so we'll add your jumper to it. Would anyone like more juice?"

"I would," Dad said as he gave his glass to Mom. "We have a lot to fit into your summer days, so Mom planned a new schedule. One thing we've decided is to start next year's math and English books. We know it's hard if we take a break from those two subjects and then try to get up to speed after not doing them for several months. Mom would also like to exercise, so a walk for all of you has been planned. Mom has some cleaning and organizing projects she wants to do—"

"Mom does a very nice job of keeping the house clean," interjected Mitch, this time making sure he wasn't talking with his mouth full.

Dad nodded. "She does. But, remember Mitch, it's not polite to interrupt. The things on Mom's list are not jobs like 'vacuum the house,' but rather tasks such as packing away the old school books, working on a school schedule, putting photos in albums, and other such items. In the new schedule, you older three will take turns watching the twins so she can have time to do school meetings and organizing. You will also have time to work on projects of your own. Next week will be free, except for learning to use your ChorePacks. We'll start the summer schedule the week after that. All right, let's get cleanup done."

Mitch stacked a pile of dishes to be rinsed next to the sink. He turned around, and Maple stood near, with her head cocked to one side and brown eyes watching Mitch intently. "What's the problem?" Mitch asked. "Did I forget to give you breakfast?" He rushed to the back room to feed the dog. Dumping a scoopful of food into her bowl, he rubbed her ears. "Good girl. You may eat."

When breakfast cleanup was finished, Mom went over Maddie's picture cards with her, since Maddie had begged to do her ChorePack. "First, you need to clip the pack to your jumper," Mom instructed, allowing Maddie to do it herself. "After you wake up in the morning, you and Mollie will take turns changing in the upstairs bathroom, and the boys will take turns in the downstairs one. You will also need to brush your hair before going to the kitchen to get your ChorePack. What's the first card show you?"

Maddie paused. "It looks like a Bible."

"Right. Since you can't read yet, you're going to start listening to the Bible on CD."

Maddie's eyes widened. "Really, Mommy?"

"Yes! Daddy bought a small CD player and also earphones for you. You'll be able to do your Bible time with all the others, listening to the Bible on CD. How would you like that?"

"I'd be so 'cited!" Maddie beamed with delight.

"What's the next card?"

"My nightgown."

"Yes! You need to put your nightgown away." Mom flipped a card. "What's this one?"

"A picture of a bed."

"Correct. You'll make your bed." Mom went through several more cards until she came to the second to last one. "I've decided you'll get to do two new jobs. The first is to wipe the bathroom sinks each day, and the second is to change out the hand towels in the bathrooms."

"I like it; thank you Mommy!" Maddie hugged Mom and then hurried off. "I'm going to do my ChorePack," she whispered to herself, rummaging through to find her nightgown card.

Around 10:30, the doorbell rang. Dad had been doing finances on the computer, but he hurried from the back room: "I'll get it." Dad was only outside for a minute, and when he came in, he was smiling. "Emily," he said to Mom, who was making Grandma's birthday cake with Mollie, "that was Mr. Delome. He has been watching the ads in the newspaper to see if any baby cribs come up for sale. He found one."

"Wonderful!" she exclaimed. "The twins are really out-growing being together; I'd be happy to have them moved into their own beds." Mom stayed home with the twins while Dad and the rest went to look at the crib. An hour and a half later, they were back with a slightly used baby bed!

After lunch, the twins' moving process began. First, it took a little while for Dad and the boys to carry the unassembled crib from the van. Mom surveyed the boys' room, pondering how they'd manage a new room setup. "I think if we move the dresser down a few feet, this would be a good spot for the crib. What do you think?"

Dad glanced where Mom was pointing. "That'll work well," he agreed.

Mollie sat on Max's bed holding Melissa. Mom had Moses in the sling, and Maddie perched on the edge of the bunk-bed ladder. "What is in this dresser?" Mitch sighed. "It feels like it's stuffed with rocks."

Max grinned. "It probably is: all the ones we brought back from our trip a few years ago."

Mitch shook his head. "Maybe we can start a rock garden outside."

"Where do you want the changing table?" Dad asked Mom.

"In the girls' room. Maddie and I will quickly clean the crib. It doesn't look dirty, but since my baby will be sleeping in it, I'd feel better if I knew it was sanitized."

Dad sorted through the plastic bag of hardware items that had come with the crib. "I hope we have all the pieces; I'll hold the footboard. Max, you can grab one side of the crib and Mitch the other."

"Then what?" Mitch wondered.

"The connector pins need to go in the hole near the bottom."

Mitch followed Dad's instructions. "Like this?"

"Yes."

Several minutes later, Mom noticed Maple was not with them. "I don't think I've seen her since we finished lunch. She might be down by her food bowl if Mitch didn't feed her."

"I almost forgot to give her breakfast, but I know I gave her lunch on time."

"I'll go find her," Maddie offered. She hurried downstairs and hopped through the living room, dining room, and kitchen, but the dog wasn't to be found. Maddie stopped to think. Maybe Maple was in the back room or laundry room. She skipped through both places and even checked under the computer desk, but no Maple.

Racing back up the stairs, the last place to look was her bedroom. There Maple was on Maddie's bed, shredding several socks with her strong, sharp teeth. Bits of pink, white, and green cotton were in a pile near Maple's front paws. Maple stopped when she saw Maddie. "Oh, Maple!" Maddie cried, picking up a few wet pieces of what used to be a sock. "Those are my socks! I'm going to tell Daddy!" Maddie rushed into the boys' room. "Maple is on my bed chewing my socks!"

"Is she really?" Dad said, stopping his work on the crib. The entire family filed into the girls' room. Maple now stood next to Maddie's bed, and a flowered sock peeked from her mouth. "Maple, drop it," Dad scolded. Maple guiltily let the sock fall at his feet. "Good drop." Dad reached for Maple's collar and walked her from the room. "You have to go to your kennel because you were chewing socks."

"It looks like you left your sock drawer open," Mitch observed. "Maple must've gone through most of your drawer!"

Maddie burst out crying. "I need my socks!"

Mom examined the extent of the damage. "It's not all of your socks, probably just three pairs. We'll get you some new ones if you need them. The last time Maple chewed socks was when she was a puppy; I thought she was past this."

"Actually," Mitch informed, "after the twins were born, she ruined a pair of Mollie's socks; we must have forgotten to tell you." He began collecting remnants of the socks. "I'll help Maddie take care of the mess."

Meanwhile, Dad and Max finished setting up the crib, and then Mom made the bed with fresh sheets. "This is your new bed," Mom told Moses. "You're going to be with the boys now."

It was time for the twins' nap, so the moving process was halted until late afternoon. After family Bible time at the end of the party that evening, Mom fed the twins. The test was at hand: how would the twins react to being in separate cribs? Mom kissed Moses and gave him to Dad. Moses' eyes were open as they stepped into the boys' room. "I can't believe we finally get him in here," Mitch sighed happily from the top bunk. "It seems I've been waiting forever!" He hopped down the ladder. "May I hold him while we pray?"

Dad nodded. After several minutes of chatting, Dad, Max, and Mitch each prayed. Mitch yawned. "I'm ready to go to sleep." He paused for a moment, looking worried. "You don't suppose Moses will cry in the night?"

"Hopefully not." Dad took Moses from Mitch. "If he does, you can get Mom or me." Dad laid the baby in the crib, and Moses' head popped up instantly. Dad tucked a blanket over him. "I know; this is a new bed," he chuckled. "You're okay. Night-night time. Daddy loves you."

Bits of pink, white, and green cotton were in a pile near Maple's front paws. Maple stopped when she saw Maddie.

Mitch crawled to the top bunk and kept a sharp eye on the baby in the dim light. As Dad left, he whispered, "He's still looking around."

"He should settle down pretty soon and go to sleep."

In the girls' room, Melissa was already asleep before Mom laid her in the crib. Mom prayed with the girls and then slipped from the room. A minute later, Maddie sat straight up in bed. "Mollie, I prayed by myself for Mrs. Parker to have a baby. Did you pray too?"

"Not yet—I forgot. Thanks for the reminder. Love you, Maddie."

"Love you too, and Melissa, I love you." Maddie's voice was beginning to sound sleepy.

Chapter 7

Testing Time

Max closed his math book with a thump. "Done!"

"Did you do that whole book today?" Maddie sat in the corner, playing with her doll.

"Oh, no. I've been working on it all year."

Mom overheard the conversation from the kitchen where she was peeling potatoes for dinner. "I'm glad you finished your math book, Max. Since this is the last day of school, I would say we cut our schedule pretty close. I usually like to finish a little earlier than this, but the twins' birth definitely impacted some school time. I am just grateful we don't have to go beyond our normal time for ending the school year."

The doorbell rang. "It's the mailman," Mitch announced. "Do you want me to get it?"

"No, I will," Mom responded, setting down a potato. "Hello," Mom said, opening the door.

There stood a short, stocky man with a bushy gray beard and round glasses. "I need a signature for the package please," the mailman's nasal voice droned.

"Isn't it a nice day?" Mom commented, handing back the green slip after signing it.

"Only for the moment. It's gonna be a very warm summer, and we don't have air conditioning in our trucks." The mailman sighed before he clomped back to his vehicle.

"Looks like a package for the twins from Aunt Olga." Mom examined the box and return address. "How kind of her to send something; when Dad's home tonight, we'll see what she sent."

That evening, Dad said Mitch could open the box, since he had been the one to call Aunt Olga when the twins were born. There were two gift-wrapped boxes inside and a note that read:

Dear Moody Family,

Congrats on M and M (I'm sure they'll like M&Ms some day. Their names escape me; I could only remember they began with an M). I imagine they're double the fun. Sorry the gift is tardy—I just don't get out and about often. Come visit me some time!

With sincerest congratulations,

Aunt Olga

Mitch moved his plate so he'd have room for the two gifts. "I'm going to open the smallest first." Mitch tore the paper off the first gift and found a box tightly sealed with strong tape. "Max, would you help me with your pocketknife?" Mitch really wanted his own knife, but Dad had said not until he was a little older.

"Sure." Max cautiously slit open the box.

"Oh, it's a toy phone." Max cut the safety ties from the back and handed the phone to Mitch. When Mitch pushed several buttons, a tune rang out.

Maddie stood near, attentively watching the process. "Open the next one, Mitch. May I please try the phone?"

Mitch handed the phone to Maddie. "Now this is a bigger one," Mitch observed, picking up the next one. He tore into the wrapping paper and opened the box. "If this is really what it shows, it's a toy momma duck and her little babies." Mitch lifted out a plastic duck with several baby ducks attached in a line behind it. "The box says 'Your toddler will learn coordination as he pulls the string and all the ducks follow him.' Let me give it a try." Mitch hopped off his chair and placed the toy on the floor. When he jerked the string, the line of ducks on wheels followed, making a "quack, quack, quack, quack, quack" noise.

Dad laughed. "What a toy!"

Later that evening, Dad found Mitch in the living room, "dialing" a phone number and listening as it played a tune. Mitch gave a tug to the duck, laughing at its funny version of "quack, quack, quack, quack, quack."

"Enjoying it?" Dad quietly asked.

Mitch jumped and turned a slight shade of red. "Baby toys are kind of fun to play with, and the twins won't be old enough for these ducks for a while."

Dad chuckled. "I know. Even parents sometimes seem to enjoy electronic gadget toys more than the children."

Thursday morning arrived: the first day of testing at Grandma's house. Dad grabbed his lunch cooler, gave Mom a kiss, and patted Maddie's head. "I want you to be Mom's helper today. She'll need a lot of help since the older ones will be gone."

"Okay, Daddy, I'll try." Maddie saw the lunch cooler. "Mommy made a special—" Maddie abruptly stopped, clapping her hand over her mouth. "I can't say."

Dad smiled. "See you tonight! Emily, I'm leaving the van with you in case you need it." Max, Mollie, and Mitch piled into the car.

"Thanks! I hope your tests go well!" Mom called. Maple stood between Mom and Maddie, her head hanging low because she had to stay home.

A little while later, Dad parked in Grandpa and Grandma's circle driveway. Grandpa stepped through the doorway. "Good morning! Are you coming to clean the house? You too, Jim?"

"Grandpa!" Mollie giggled.

"You know," Mitch said as he closed the car door behind him. "Grandma's going to test us!"

"Oh, yes." Grandpa's eyes twinkled. "Speaking of cleaning, Mitch, I've been cleaning bathrooms ever since we helped you all after the twins were born. Grandma is shocked when she finds the bathroom clean!"

"You have?" Mitch's eyes widened.

"Sure have. Helping at your house motivated me to practice my new skills at home, and Grandma's thrilled to have me help her. I can clean a bathroom quite well now. But while you test how smart you are, I'm going to work."

"Oh, I forgot you have to work some days," Max said.

"I know. Work was slow this spring, which was great since we helped at your house. I'll be working three days a week over the summer. Say, do you boys remember Marvin Jones, the wallpaper man?" Grandpa asked. Max and Mitch nodded. "I called and invited him to lunch today. If you think about it, please pray. He and his wife were having marriage problems in December when we talked, and I'm going to share about the Lord with him."

"We'll pray," Dad stated. "By the way, do you have a moving date?"

"Sort of. The guy who is living there now will be moving out this weekend," Grandpa said. "Since this house hasn't sold and we'll be doing projects at the new house, I'm not feeling a push to get moved. Plus, it'll take time to pack, and with my working several days a week and doing house things the afternoons I'm off, it'll be a busy summer. My plan is to move in August, although Grandma isn't thrilled because it'll be hot."

Grandpa and Dad left for work, and the children went inside. Grandma was finishing up the breakfast dishes. "I'm glad to see your three happy faces this morning," she said as she gave each of them a hug.

"The 'For Sale' sign is new in your yard," Max commented.

"Yes, the realtor put it up after we met with him the other day."

The children chatted with Grandma for several minutes, until she left to bring out the testing booklets. She handed each child a booklet with the questions and a paper where they would fill in their answers. "We're going to start with the Language Skills section. Make sure your pencils say they are number two pencils; I told your mom that was what you would need."

"We have them," Mitch assured her. "Although I don't understand why the number two matters."

"I think they're a special type of lead," Grandma explained, "and they must need that for the machines to read your answers." She went over the test instructions, which included encouragement to go slowly and double-check answers if there was time. Finally, Grandma set her watch for thirty-five minutes and said, "You may begin."

The room was quiet, except for the slight scratching of pencils and the hum of the air conditioner outside the window. When Max turned his page, Mitch felt frustrated. *Why is Max always faster?* He sighed and gnawed the end of his pencil. "Don't chew on the pencil," Max whispered. Mitch meekly nodded, continuing with his test.

Grandma sat near Mollie with a stack of note cards. She picked one from the pile, and her pen was soon moving along the card. A few minutes passed, and Mitch tipped his head back. *I wonder how tall Grandpa's ceiling is,* he thought to himself. *Dad would know.* His eye caught a swift movement. *That's a big spider, and he's motoring along pretty good. I hope he doesn't drop down, because I don't like spiders.*

Mollie could tell Mitch was watching something, so she naturally followed his gaze. "SPIDER!" she shouted, scooting back from the table.

"Where?!" Grandma's voice sounded several tones higher than normal as she jumped up on her chair. One thing Grandma detested was spiders.

"It's right above you," Max answered for Mitch and pointed to the black fuzzy spider with arched legs.

"Oh, no!" Grandma almost fell scrambling off the chair. "I should've asked where it was before I chose my route of escape." While they watched, the fast-moving spider repelled off the ceiling. Grandma, Mollie, and Mitch instinctively backed up several steps.

"I found his rope!" Max grabbed for the spider's string. When he pulled the string up, the spider came up. When he lowered the string, the spider went down. "He has a white spot on his head," Max announced, "and his hairy fur makes him look a—" Just then, the spider rapidly scaled the string, and as Max let go, the string broke.

"Please, Max, kill that spider," Grandma begged, watching the spider rapidly scurry across the floor.

"Sure, Grandma." Max took care of the spider and then used a paper towel to carry it to the trash. "Sorry, Grandma. I shouldn't have played with him."

"At least he didn't run for me! You all may go back to your test."

The phone rang, and Grandma stepped from the room to answer it. By the time she returned, the children had completed their tests. "That was our realtor, Gary Olson—"

"Grandma!" Mitch interrupted. "He's the same guy you bought the house from! Oops. Sorry, I'm not supposed to interrupt."

"We liked the realtor so well we asked if he could list this one," Grandma explained. "Anyway, Gary said he wanted to drop by with two people in about forty-five minutes and show our house. He apologized for such short notice, but he said I could stay here. I told him I was giving standardized tests to my homeschooled grandchildren. We should be able to finish our next test before he comes."

When the realtor arrived, the children had completed their test and were ready for a break. They could hear him talking to his clients. "The reason they're moving is because they want to be next door to their grandkids; you know, to spoil them."

Another voice was talking, but it was too soft to understand. Mr. Olson continued: "One of the biggest benefits to the house is the living room; it's just huge. When your family expands with spouses and grandchildren, and you host family gatherings, you need a place for everyone to fit."

The man laughed. "You're already selling me on it."

"I haven't finished," Mr. Olson protested mildly. "The large windows overlook a two-acre backyard, and it would be a perfect location for a small pond. The bay windows are simply elegant and spacious, great to sit by and read a book on a cold, winter day or sunny afternoon."

Grandma collected the children's answer booklets into a pile. "Mitch, you may pick two things in the pantry for our snack. I just realized I forgot to water my garden this morning, so we'll take a few minutes to do that."

"Yes, ma'am." Mitch hopped off his chair and headed for the pantry. Walking through the kitchen, he suddenly stopped.

Mr. Olson was in the hall, with his back to Mitch, but he was saying, "We'll look at the bedrooms later; I want to show you the part Clara will like." Mitch dove for the pantry, opened the door, and paused. He didn't want to distract from the house tour by being found in the kitchen when they came to look at it. *Should he close the pantry door or leave it open?* He heard footsteps, and he knew time was short. In the dim light, he spied Grandma's aprons hanging in the corner. They wouldn't provide enough of a hiding place. The only option: open the pantry door, stand behind it, and hope they didn't look there. This was accomplished, and a short moment later, footsteps approached the pantry. Mitch's heart beat wildly in his chest. *I wonder if I should have gone back to the dining room; I don't want to embarrass anyone.* Mr. Olson was saying, "Now this is what I call a spacious pantry."

The man chuckled. "Only Clara cares about that: she's a good cook, and when she shops, you'd better beware!"

Mr. Olson felt for the light switch while Mitch's heart sank. "What a nice place to hang brooms," the lady's voice commented as the light came on. Mitch saw a movement and cautiously turning his head, he noticed a hand grip the side of the door. *Oh, no!* he thought. *What should I say if I'm found?* Grinning to himself, he figured the polite thing would be: *Hello, I'm Mitch. What would you like for a snack?*

The hand disappeared, as Mr. Olson continued, "If you're ready, we'll head for the garage."

Mitch waited until he was certain they were safely in the garage, and then he stepped out from behind the door. *Mr. Olson forgot to turn off the light,* Mitch thought, swiftly choosing two snacks. He didn't want to risk them coming back and being stuck in the pantry while they toured the kitchen and dining room!

Mitch hurried to the backyard to find the rest. Grandma and Mollie stood on the edge of the small garden while Max

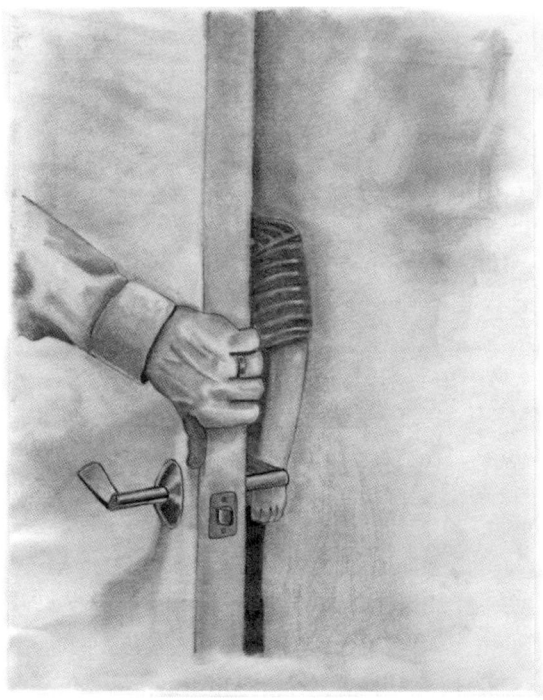

Mitch saw a movement and cautiously turning his head, he noticed a hand grip the side of the door.

watered it. "Your tomato plants are looking good," Mollie complimented Grandma as she fingered a leaf. "I wanted a garden, but with the twins, it didn't work out this year. Mom said we might be able to next summer. We did plant sunflowers last week, and I'm looking forward to watching them grow."

"Grandma," Max changed the subject. "We've been talking about Father's Day and what gift to get for Dad, but we've only had one idea. Do you have any? He's your son!"

Grandma laughed. "Yes, he is, but he hasn't been living with us for many years, so I don't know him as well. What about making a birdhouse?"

Max sighed. "I suggested that already, but Mitch didn't like it."

"Sometimes I run dry of ideas for Grandpa, and I give him clothes. Hi, Mitch! Did you find the snacks?"

"Yes, but you'll never believe what happened!"

After Mitch told the story, Grandma shook her head. "I should have thought they could come that way although it really wouldn't have mattered if they had seen you. If they had found you in the pantry, they would have been very surprised, and you all would have had a good laugh."

Max turned off the nozzle. "I think that should do it."

The four went back into the house, and Mitch showed them the snacks. "Good," Max remarked. "These are my favorite crackers."

"Plus chips!" Mitch opened the bag, popping a chip into his mouth.

Mr. Olson and his clients walked into the kitchen, and after several minutes of talking, the realtor stepped into the dining room while the couple continued a discussion in the kitchen.

"Sorry to interrupt you here; thanks for the graciousness of letting us drop in so unexpectedly," Mr. Olson said. His blond hair was swept back off his forehead, and he was sharply dressed in casual khaki pants and a button-up shirt.

"Mr. Olson," Max started, "do you know why the house has been empty across the street from us—the one next to Mr. Delome's? It doesn't even have a 'For Sale' sign anymore."

Mr. Olson waved a hand. "The owner changed his mind on selling it for now: I don't know what he's going to do with the place, but he dropped his listing. The house your grand-parents bought is a much nicer one."

Mr. Olson's clients walked in, and the wife exclaimed over the dining room. "This is just what we're looking for!"

The man, dressed in blue jeans and a striped polo shirt, patted Max. "How is that finger doing, Maxwell?" The only person Max could remember who called him by his full name over the past year was Dr. Rex, when he had stitched up his finger. Max recognized his face, although he looked very different not being in doctor's scrubs.

"I didn't know you at first, Dr. Rex! It doesn't hurt at all any-more, and there's just a small scar."

Dr. Rex folded his arms across his chest. "Glad to hear that."

"How did you remember my name with so many patients?"

"I have a way with names. Also, since your dad manages my trust fund, it's easier to remember you, because you all come up in conversation, and your family picture is on his desk."

"I didn't know doctors could be off in the middle of the week."

Dr. Rex laughed. "I was on emergency call last weekend, so I have two weekdays off. Another doctor is taking my place."

Clara, Dr. Rex's wife, had a sweet disposition. "We're looking for a home closer to Rex's work," she explained. "We live really far out in the country, and although I still want to live in the country, I'd rather not be so far away. Rex finally had time to house hunt with me."

A cell phone was ringing, and it was the doctor's. He pulled it from his pocket, glancing at the screen. "I'll be back," he said, and he stepped onto the deck. A minute later, Dr. Rex burst in the door. "I hate to do this to you, Clara, but there's been an emergency, and I need to get to the hospital. We'll have to finish the tour later." With a wave to the Moodys and Gary Olson, Dr. Rex and his wife hurried from the room.

Mr. Olson smiled. "You never know what might come up. Thank you for letting us intrude on your morning, Mrs. Moody. I'd better be going myself."

Mollie crunched on a chip. "I wonder what sort of emergency it was."

"Maybe someone needed surgery," Mitch suggested.

"I didn't think he did surgeries." Max counted ten crackers and arranged them in a circle.

"Well, whatever it is, he had to leave; I think they would be nice people to buy our house." Grandma opened her teacher's guide. "Was the last test hard?"

"No," Max spoke for the three.

"I'm glad. We'll do one more before lunch, and then see how many we can fit in this afternoon."

Chapter 8

New Schedule

Beep, beep, beep, beep. The persistent noise continued until Max realized his watch alarm was going off. *That's right; today's the first day of our new summer schedule,* he thought. Maple's wet nose brushed his hand, and her tail thumped vigorously against the bed. "I guess you heard my alarm too. Good girl," he said in a low voice while he held Maple's body away from the bed so her tail wagging wouldn't make too much noise and wake up Moses. Then Max remembered Mom was feeding the twins, and Moses wasn't even in his crib.

Scooting from his bed, he tugged on Mitch's sheet. "Mitch. It's time to wake up! We're going to have our Bible reading and prayer in the living room so Moses can sleep when Mom brings him back."

When no response was heard, Max realized Mitch wasn't in the bed. *He must have gotten up early,* Max chuckled to himself. Hurrying from the room, with Maple following closely behind, he almost bumped into Mitch at the bottom of the stairs. "You're up early!" Max exclaimed.

"I know—I was excited about our new schedule."

Dad looked up from reading his Bible. "Good morning, Max," Dad greeted him. "I'm glad to see you are up on time!" Maple bounded toward Dad, her tail whirling in circles as she reached him. "I know. Nice to see you too," said Dad, scratching her ears.

Max let Maple outside and then went to change in the bathroom. He was grateful he had remembered to put his clothes there the night before. When he was done, Maple was ready to come back in, and he found his ChorePack in the kitchen. *Mine is the only one left,* Max thought to himself. *I saw Mitch had his, and the girls must have grabbed theirs!*

Mollie and Mitch sat on the couch, silently reading their Bibles. Dad was helping Maddie learn how to work the new CD player. It was to be her first morning listening to the Bible on CD. Her face glowed as Dad showed her what button started the CD and how she could pause it when she was done. After Maddie successfully started the CD, Dad helped her put in the earphones.

Several minutes later, Mitch said, "Remember when I was grumbling about doing dinner cleanup while the girls planted sunflowers?" Dad nodded. "Well, you talked to me about the Israelites complaining in Numbers. I decided to start reading that book to learn more. They didn't trust the Lord to take care of them, but they complained about almost everything, even their food and water. The Lord disciplined them for their complaining. I needed to see how serious murmuring and being dissatisfied is. As I have gone through Numbers, I have had on my mind my bad attitude regarding that cleanup, and I've been working on not complaining."

"You're right, Son. I'm glad you decided to read there, and even more importantly, you're thinking about what you're reading. I also delight in you all being here in the living room with me for morning Bible time."

Max smiled. "I like it too; it's just hard not to talk. I've thought of two things I've wanted to say that aren't related to my Bible reading!"

Around seven, Dad patted Maddie, and she took one of the earphones out. "Your time is up, and you are Mommy's breakfast helper now. I think you forgot to brush your hair, so go ahead and do that, and Mom will be here soon." At 7:15, individual Bible time was over, and Dad stood up. "I hope you will have good attitudes and help Mom with the twins while I'm at work."

"We will," Mitch assured him, glancing down at his ChorePack. "What are we having for breakfast? Mom only came down a little while ago, and if we were having muffins or something, she would have started them earlier."

"Guess you'll find out," Dad said mysteriously, putting his Bible away.

After a special first-day-of-a-new-schedule breakfast of powdered-sugar donuts (which were greatly enjoyed), Dad left for work. In the meantime, the children did their ChorePacks since the twins were now awake. Mollie and Maddie's last chore card was to see if the sunflowers needed water, and if they did, to water them. The girls excitedly observed the tender, green plants after Maddie had soaked them in water. "They're really growing," Mollie remarked. "I think we're scheduled for a walk next; let's go wait out front for the rest."

When they arrived in the front yard, Mitch was sitting on the driveway, with Maple next to him. "I'm glad you're bringing Maple; she loves her walks." Mollie patted the dog.

"She sure does," agreed Mitch. "Didn't you like doing your ChorePack? It helped me do all my chores, without forgetting any."

"I liked it too!" Mollie nodded.

Several minutes later, the Moodys were walking by Mrs. Bagwell's house, and she lifted a bedroom window open. "Hold on for a minute." The window closed, and she soon appeared in a bathrobe, slippers, and large pink curlers. "It's

Mollie and Maddie's last chore card was to see if the sun-flowers needed water, and if they did, to water them.

nice to see you folks getting exercise on this gorgeous morning. You're quite adventuresome with the twins and the dog. You'd better keep a good grip on him, Match."

"Yes, ma'am; I will," Mitch assured Mrs. Bagwell. "Maple's pretty excited, because she loves walks."

"Well, the only reason I interrupted your walk was to tell you that I'm going to visit my daughter, and I need someone to pick up my mail and papers while I'm away."

"We'll be happy to," Mom said. She pulled back the sun shade to check on the twins.

Mrs. Bagwell sighed. "I dislike traveling—especially by myself. But, my daughter says it's important I see her, so who can argue with one's own daughter?"

"It would be hard to go alone," Mom agreed as she glanced at the stroller, hearing the start of a cry from a twin. "What day are you leaving?"

"The 21st and then I'll be home the 28th."

"Hopefully it'll be a nice break from everyday life." Mom tried to focus on her conversation with Mrs. Bagwell as she glanced down to see which twin was unhappy. "What are your plans for Snickers?" Snickers was Mrs. Bagwell's pet rat, which the Moody children had pet-sat twice. Mom hoped Snickers didn't need to be watched. She remembered the time when Snickers had disappeared from his cage, and it made her shudder to think of Snickers running loose near one of the twins.

"I'm bringing him."

Mom bent over and unbuckled Melissa. Several tears slid down the baby's cheeks. "It's okay, Melissa."

"She's a cute one," Mrs. Bagwell observed. "Not many people get to have two at a time."

"I know; we didn't deserve them."

"I'll let you resume your walk; I need to have me a session with my sweeper."

"See you later," Mom waved, and they continued on their way, with Max pushing the stroller. "I'm wishing I had brought my sling," Mom commented, "because I'm not sure Melissa is going to let me put her back in the stroller."

As soon as Mitch felt Mrs. Bagwell wouldn't be able to hear them, he blurted, "Mom, what did she mean by having a session with her sweeper?!"

"Sweeper is another name for a vacuum. It's an old-fashioned term I've occasionally heard elderly people use."

"I thought she was going to sweep her house," Mitch observed, "but didn't know how she would do it with carpet."

"Mrs. Bagwell might be onto a business idea for you all," Mom said, switching Melissa to an upright position. "The idea would be to get people's mail and papers when they're away on a trip."

"I like that," Mollie agreed.

"The only part I'm not sure about is what to do with magazines. At this time of year, catalogs often have people with swimming suits on their covers." The children were quiet as Mom pondered the thought. "I'll run this by Dad, but I think it would work if you would put the mail in a bag as you take it from the mailbox; that way, you wouldn't see anything."

The rest of the walk was spent discussing the 4th of July plans. Mom patted Melissa as she talked. "Dad said he's going to grill sausage. When we grocery shop, we can pick out several different kinds. I've thought if we ask everyone to bring a dish, we can set things out buffet style. What do you think?"

"I like the idea," Max agreed. "There would be variety, and we wouldn't have to make all the food then."

"What about drinks?" Mitch wondered.

"We should provide those. We'll have to decide what we want to offer. As we have time this week, we'll make up our guest list and then create invitations."

Around 8:45, they arrived home, thirsty and warm. Mollie poured everyone glasses of ice-cold water while Mom consulted the schedule. "The twins will have blanket time," she said, "with Max watching them in the living room. I'm going to take a quick shower. Mollie, Mitch, and Maddie may play outside until it's time to work in the yard at nine-thirty. Max, you may join them at nine when I nurse the twins."

"Mom, what will we do with that half hour after we finish all the weeding projects?" Mitch wondered.

"Dad had a few more things on a list like trimming the bushes, keeping the grass watered, and such, and then he also wants Maple brushed often. She's looking pretty scraggly."

Maple found an air conditioning vent in the kitchen and laid against it. Her pink tongue hung from the side of her mouth. Max helped Mom settle the twins on a blanket, and then Mom went to take her shower. Moses and Melissa lay several inches apart on their tummies. Melissa lifted her head up high. "Wow, Melissa!" Max exclaimed. "Good job; you're getting strong!"

Moses kicked his legs and raised his head slightly, but not as much as Melissa. "Keep working at it, Moses," encouraged Max. "I think Melissa's doing a mini push-up!" *They are cute,* he thought to himself. *Thank You Lord for giving us these babies.*

A little later, Mom came for the twins to feed them. "Mom," Max began, "I saw Melissa do something for the first time! She did a mini push-up." Max described to Mom what she was doing.

"She's probably not far from rolling over. Thank you for watching them."

Max carried Melissa upstairs for Mom, and then he went downstairs. "I'm going outside," he said aloud. Max laughed as he caught sight of Maple. "You think you've recovered enough to come with me?" Maple jumped up and wagged her tail. "Come on!" Max urged, putting Maple's collar and leash on.

Mollie, Mitch, and Maddie were riding their bicycles. "Get yours!" Mitch called.

Max looked at Maple. "I'd better brush her; Dad said she needs it. I'll just watch you from the shade of the tree."

A little before nine-thirty, Max stood up, brushing clumps of dog hair off him. "Maple is sure shedding. You all need to put away your bikes because we have to grab some tools for our weeding."

Mitch led the way to the garage and carefully slipped from his bike. "I do like to ride bikes! What tools should we get?"

"Probably a trash bag and a few small hand shovels," Max said.

The children walked to the backyard, closing the gate so Maple wouldn't escape. Mom had said they should tackle the mulched area in the corner. Maddie pulled the top off a dandelion. "Here's a pretty yellow flower. I'll give it to Mommy."

"Dandelions might be nice looking, but they're weeds," Mitch explained to Maddie. "You have to make sure to get weeds by the roots, otherwise they will come right back." Mitch removed the rest of Maddie's dandelion.

"These aren't easy weeds to deal with." Max yanked at a stubborn leafy string of green.

"Tell me about it." Mitch grasped a thick weed and pulled hard. "What I'm wondering is what we should get Dad for Father's Day."

"I don't know, but there's not much time left. Father's Day is next Sunday!"

"I have an idea," Mollie announced. "How about a tie?"

Mitch shook his head. "He already has one."

"I know he does, but this one would be different. It would have Scripture on it. I've seen Pastor Thompson wear one. We could ask him where he bought his."

"I think a Scripture tie will be our gift." Max decided, moving over a few feet. At ten, they went into the house.

"How did your weeding go?" Mom wondered.

"We made good progress." Max washed his hands in the kitchen sink. "There's still a lot to do."

"Mom," Mitch said, "Father's Day is coming, and we've been trying to decide what to purchase for Dad. We'd like to buy him a tie with Scripture on it. Mollie remembers seeing Pastor Thompson wear one, so may Max call Pastor Thompson to ask where he bought it?"

"Sure; I think Dad would like that. Okay, what do we have next?" Mom consulted the schedule. "Mollie and Mitch are going to watch the twins, Max and I will have a meeting in the dining room to go over his math and English, and Maddie will play alone in her bedroom. Max, you may make the phone call after we're done."

Mom handed a white cloth to Mitch. "I only burped Melissa, so you can do Moses."

Mitch took the offered item and sat on the couch. "I've never done this, but it doesn't seem like the cloth will help much." He fingered the thin material.

"I'll let you use two, how's that?" Mom laid the other cloth on Mitch's shoulder and handed Moses to him. "Just keep him upright—like this—and gently pat his back."

"How long?" Mitch wondered if his arms would make it.

"About five minutes, and then you may lay him on the blanket, or keep holding him. Mollie, this is the twins' time to stay awake, so if they begin to fall asleep, you'll need to pick them up. Max and I'll be in the dining room, so ask me if you need anything. Remember, Mollie, we don't want you walking the stairs holding a baby, and Mitch, the same for you."

"Yes, ma'am," Mollie agreed. She noticed a car pull into Mr. Delome's driveway. A man in a T-shirt and blue jeans, with a shaved head, jumped from a shiny, red jeep. He opened the back cargo door, and a German shepherd leapt out. Mr.

Delome stood on the front porch, smiling, and then the three disappeared inside the house.

"Mr. Delome seems to know who the man is," Mitch said, straining to see from where he was sitting. "But I don't." Mitch realized he was forgetting to pat Moses, so he resumed his job.

"Oh, I know!" Mollie nodded. "It's his son. He told Dad recently his son was coming." Several minutes later, movement outside caught Mollie's attention, and she looked up. "Wasn't the son's name Bill? Yes, I guess it was. Bill just went to his jeep. This time he has on a hat. He wore that ball cap all the time when he was visiting Mr. Delome after Thanksgiving."

Melissa squealed, surprising Mollie. "I didn't know you were unhappy!" Mollie remarked. She picked a toy out of the toy tub. "Look, Melissa." Mollie vigorously shook the rattle, and Melissa stuck her thumb in her mouth. "How cute! Mitch, Melissa's sucking her thumb for the first time!"

A little before ten-thirty, Mom and Max were done, and it was time for the twins' nap. Max helped Mom bring them to bed. Mom came down a few minutes later with the hand-held baby monitor. Since the twins were in separate rooms, Dad had purchased a baby video monitor set. One camera was in Melissa's room and the other in Moses'. Mom could watch the babies on the small screen and hear them if there was a problem. The monitor switched back and forth between the two rooms. "Melissa was sucking her thumb again, Mollie," Mom said. "I heard you tell Mitch she had, and when I laid her in the bed, she stuck it right in. This is a day of firsts for her: she was doing a baby push-up during blanket time! What does the schedule say we are to do next?"

Max read the 10:30 time slot. "You have a meeting with Mollie for fifteen minutes; Mitch showers, and I do English.

Then, after Mollie's done, Mitch has a meeting, and Mollie showers. Maddie will do coloring books now and then puzzles at eleven."

Mom and Mollie sat side by side on the couch and read through Mollie's math lesson, using a small whiteboard to work the practice problems. When her time was up, Mitch was next. Mom spent a half hour on her organizing projects before needing to wake the twins at eleven-thirty.

"I like babies, Mommy," Maddie remarked, smoothing out a blanket she had put on the floor for the twins. "Oh! Moses' sock is gone."

"It probably came off in bed," Mom decided. "Or maybe when Max carried him down."

"I'll check." Maddie was glad for an opportunity to be helpful.

"What were you working on today for organizing?" Max wondered.

"Packing away all the completed school books. It shouldn't take me more than two or three days."

A minute later, Maddie was back with the missing sock. "It was next to his bed; if Maple had been in there, she would have ated it!"

"You mean eaten," Mom gently corrected.

"Yes."

Max's time with Maddie and the twins went quickly. At noon, Mom came for the twins to feed them, and Mollie and Mitch prepared a simple lunch of sandwiches and fruit. They put the sandwich fixings and fruit in the refrigerator until Mom was ready, and they had free time before lunch.

After lunch cleanup, Max practiced the piano while Mollie worked on a letter to Aunt Olga, and Mitch studied his plumbing book. A few minutes before one-thirty, the children hurried to prepare to go to Grandpa and Grandma's new house. "Do we need to bring anything?" Mitch asked Max.

"I don't know; Grandpa hasn't mentioned it."

Mom glanced up from the book she was reading to Maddie. "You can always come home to get things if you need to." Moses was snuggled in Mom's arms, and Melissa was nearby on the blanket.

"Hurry, Mollie, wherever you are!" Max called. "We're going to be a minute late!"

Mollie almost fell down the stairs in her haste. "Sorry! I was having trouble getting my hair into a ponytail."

After the children left, Mom said to Maddie, "I'll let you hold Moses for a few minutes if you sit right here."

Maddie's face brightened. "Okay, Mommy. I'll hold Moses, and you can hold Melissa. We'll both be holding babies!"

Chapter 9

Projects and Father's Day

Grandpa and Grandma's new house was ranch-style, and although it was smaller than the one they were moving from, it would be quite adequate. The three children stood on the steps, waiting for Grandpa or Grandma to answer the door. "Hi," Grandma smiled at them. "Come on in!"

Grandpa was in the kitchen, swiftly scribbling on a piece of paper. "I thought we needed a list of all the projects to be done. I'm a little surprised myself at what I came up with. I'll read it to you. Fix nail holes and other dings before painting, paint all the rooms, install new smoke detectors, shampoo carpet, clean the fireplace, wash windows, replace the glass storm door, replace locks on the front and back doors, vacuum out cupboards in kitchen and bathrooms, put shelf liners in all the cabinets, take shower doors outside to clean, re-caulk some seams in the showers—oh, and fix the leaky faucet in the bathroom." Grandpa paused. "I expect to come up with more as we work."

"Grandpa!" Mitch exclaimed. "We've fixed a leaky faucet before, and I've been reading about that in my plumbing book. I could fix the faucet all by myself!"

"That'll be perfect," Grandpa agreed, looking up from his list. "We'll see what supplies you might need, and we'll plan on you doing the project sometime this week.

"I hope they gave you a discount on the house." Max seemed serious. "That's a lot to fix!"

"They gave what they called a paint allowance," Grandpa said, setting his pen down. "Which means they knew the house needed to be painted, so they gave a small discount to help with the paint costs. Martha, I thought you and Mollie could start on the cabinet cleaning."

"Sure, James."

"Boys, we'll replace the locks on the front and back doors. I didn't think to tell you to bring tools, but I have two screwdrivers, so we'll be okay. When you leave today, we will evaluate what we will do tomorrow so you know what tools to bring."

Grandpa and the boys walked to the front door. It was oak with a decorative glass cut-out in the middle of the top half. "Have you ever installed a lock before?" Grandpa asked them.

"No, I don't think we have," Max decided.

"Then this'll be a great learning opportunity." Grandpa rummaged through a plastic bag, retrieving the lock package. With some effort, Grandpa worked his way into the child-proof packaging that surrounded the lock. After skimming the instructions, he said, "The first thing is to remove the two screws on the back of the lock. Then, pull the two halves apart."

The boys followed Grandpa's directions; after the screws were removed, they carefully pulled the metal pieces apart. "Good," Grandpa affirmed. "You'll need to unscrew the plate on the side of the door. Normally, if you can get the same lock brand, you don't need to replace it, but I wasn't able to find a match."

As Mitch worked, he said, "Grandpa, guess what we're going to get Dad for Father's Day?"

"A puppy?"

"Grandpa! No, we already have a dog. Maybe for your Father's Day gift Grandma can get you one!"

Grandpa chuckled. "I doubt she would, but I'd enjoy it. So, what did you buy?"

"We ordered him a tie. I can't wait to see him wear it."

"You can never have enough ties." Grandpa nodded approvingly. "So the side plate is off. Max, look in the package. There should be two different plates—one with square edges and the other with rounded. We need the rounded one."

"Grandpa, what is Grandma bringing to our 4th of July picnic?" Max wondered, finding the piece Grandpa had asked for. "I hope it's something wonderful."

Grandpa laughed. "You can count on it. I don't know what she's planned, but if she doesn't have time, I can always run to the bakery for cinnamon rolls." Soon, the new lock was installed.

In the kitchen, Grandma and Mollie were working. "This is awfully dusty, and this one has food crumbs all over," Grandma exclaimed, peeking in a cupboard. "I'm glad we don't have ants to deal with."

Mollie plugged the vacuum in. "Where would you like me to start?"

"Probably at the far end. I think the skinny attachment will be the best one to use." Mollie popped the attachment on the end of the vacuum hose. *This is a really long cabinet,* she thought to herself, turning on the vacuum. The first project afternoon flew by, and the children had enjoyed their time. Grandpa remarked about how much they had accomplished, how thankful they were for the help, and how there was plenty to keep them busy for a while!

The rest of the week, whenever the children had free time, they worked on Father's Day plans and making 4th of July invitations. One afternoon, Max sat on the piano bench. "Okay," he said and began flipping through the hymn book. "If you really think we can do this for Dad, we'll have to find a simple hymn, so I have a better possibility of playing it."

Mollie plunked several keys. "You're better than I am, that's for sure."

"How about 'Jesus Loves Me'?" Mitch suggested. "It's an easy one to sing."

"Let me look." Max glanced in the index and turned to the correct page. "Dad's going to be surprised with this."

Maddie climbed up on the bench and pushed several keys. "See, Max? I can play too. Maybe we can play together."

"That's called a duet," Mitch informed her. "But I don't think you can play a duet yet. I'm still learning myself."

"Max," Mollie started, "shouldn't we call Mr. Parker to tell him we're going to sing at church on Sunday?"

"We probably should; I'll ask Mom if we can."

Friday after lunch, the children had another idea: they would make a special Father's Day card with the twins' hands outlined on the front. Mollie took a piece of heavy white cardstock paper, and she folded it in half. Mom sat down on a chair with Moses, and Melissa was nearby in the swing. "I remember doing this with Max when he was a baby," Mom reminisced. "Instead of doing it this way, I wanted to get a handprint, so I used ink. He ended up getting the ink on his clothes and me. Oh, it was a mess. Tracing hands is a better way to go." Mom leaned closer to the paper, gently directing Moses' hand to a good position. "Moses, you're going to do this for your daddy," Mom encouraged, trying to hold his little hand still. Max grabbed a pencil and began tracing. Half way through, Moses lifted his fingers, as if to touch the pencil. Mom attempted to help him flatten his hand, but he curled his fingers.

Maddie stood nearby, observing the process. "Why won't he listen to you?" she wondered. "He's supposed to obey just like me."

"Moses is too young to obey like you," Mom explained. "As he gets older, he'll understand."

After a few more tries, both of Moses' hands had been traced, and he had seemed to almost enjoy it. Mom glanced at Melissa because she was beginning to cry. Mom handed Moses to Max and unbuckled Melissa. "Mitch, you may try tracing Melissa's hand while Max holds Moses," Mom instructed, glad that Melissa's crying had lessened.

Mom guided Melissa's hand to the paper. As Mitch traced it, several tears dropped onto the paper and smudged the pencil lead. Maddie giggled. "That was one of her crying tears, Mommy, but she's only a little bit unhappy now!"

Finally, the project was accomplished, and the children worked on writing individual greetings inside the card to Dad. They even wrote a note as if it were from the twins.

Saturday, after the twins' naps, the Moodys distributed their 4th of July invitations, along with a plate of homemade frosted star sugar cookies. All of the neighbors they invited seemed very interested.

Sunday morning arrived, and the children were up early. Mom, Mollie, and Maddie had gone grocery shopping on Saturday for a special outing together, and they had purchased the necessary ingredients for Dad's breakfast: eggs, hash browns, and store-bought biscuits from a can. Mollie and Mitch had decorated the house with signs that had mes-

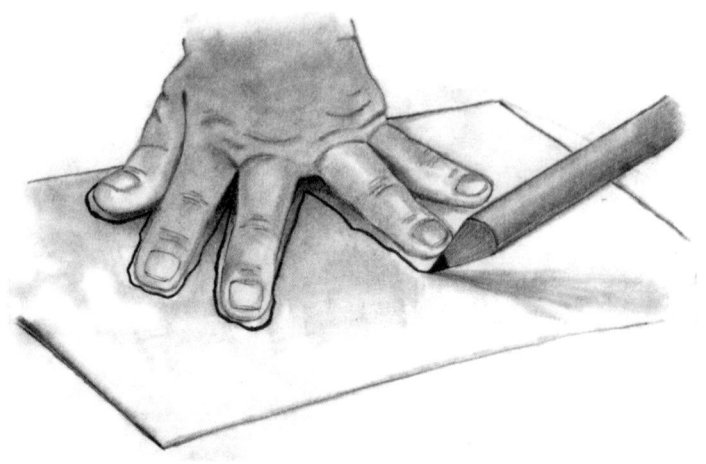

Max grabbed a pencil and began tracing.

sages such as "The Best Dad in the World" and "We love you, Dad" and "Dad loves Jesus!"

A few minutes later, Dad joined them in the dining room. "Thank you, children, for the Father's Day signs. I noticed them right away, and I've been reading them. I don't deserve a bit of what you all are doing, but you've made me feel very loved."

"We worked on them in the afternoons," replied Mollie. "When are you going to open your presents?"

"Would you please do them now?" Mitch pleaded.

Dad glanced at the clock. "Maybe. Let me bless the food first."

After Dad prayed, he came back to the question at hand. "It seems we are a little earlier than normal for a Sunday, and we would have time to do the presents now. What do you think, Emily?"

"Now would be fine. We're having Grandpa and Grandma over at lunch, and then we're helping with the special service and dinner at church tonight."

Mollie hurried from the room and brought in two packages. "This one is from us children," she announced, handing it to Dad.

Dad felt the package. "I think it's a box." He shook it. "I wonder if you disguised something."

Mitch almost burst with excitement, yet he kept his mouth closed. Dad tore off the paper and saw a brown box. His eyes twinkled. "I guessed right! Where's your handy pocketknife, Max?"

Max quickly produced the knife and carefully slit the box open. "Thanks, Max. A tie!" Dad exclaimed with pleasure. "How did you know I needed a new one?"

"It has Bible verses on it," Maddie informed.

"Quiet, Maddie!" Mitch exclaimed, shooting a disapproving look at her.

"Sorry."

"I hadn't noticed that part yet." Dad examined the tan-colored tie. John 3:16 was printed on it with black lettering. "This'll be a perfect work tie. How did you find a tie with Scripture?"

"Because," Mitch began, "we saw Pastor Thompson wear one, and we asked him where he bought it. Did you see his?"

Dad shook his head. "No, I didn't."

"Maddie, please forgive me for giving you a bad look a minute ago," Mitch requested.

"I forgive you."

After Dad opened a gift from Mom, which was a new watch, Mom left to feed the twins while the others cleaned up breakfast and prepared for church. The morning seemed to drag by slowly; the children could hardly wait until their special music! Mr. Parker had told the children they should sing their song after Grandpa took prayer requests. As Grandpa wrote down the requests, Max whispered to Mitch, "I'm getting nervous. Do you have the song book?"

"Yes, it's behind Mrs. Parker's book on the piano. Don't be nervous."

"I am." Max showed Mitch his hands, which shook slightly.

Maddie sat next to Dad and Mom in the front, and upon hearing the boys whisper, she turned around. "Are we ready?" she loudly asked.

Dad patted Maddie. "It's prayer time."

When Grandpa was through, Mitch jumped up with Max, Mollie, and Maddie following him. "Please stay where you are, Jim," Grandpa announced. "The children are going to do something."

Max slid onto the piano bench, reaching for his book. Mrs. Parker's song book slid down and hit the keys with an unmelodious crash. Max's face turned a slight red while Mitch ignored the distraction. "Dad, we're going to sing you a song," he declared. "We're not professionals, but I hope you like it."

Mitch nodded at Max, who faltered through an introduction. "Jesus loves me this I know," the three voices sang, "for the Bible tells me so. Little ones to Him belong, they are weak but He is strong."

At the end, Dad's eyes were filled with tears, and he gave each one a hug. "Thank you!" he exclaimed as everyone gave the children a round of applause. "What a special Father's Day gift!"

Chapter 10 | Baking Business and the 4th of July

One morning the week after Father's Day, the phone rang, and Max answered it. "It's Miss Jenkins for you, Mollie."

Mollie hurried to the phone and talked for a few minutes. "Miss Jenkins wants me to make cookies for her to bring to a family get-together; I made gingersnaps for her last year. I'm so happy I can do my baking business again!"

At lunch, Mom wrote out a grocery list of items they would need for their 4th of July picnic. "I wonder how much juice we'll go through." Mom tapped her pen thoughtfully on the paper. "Max, would you please grab our guest list and count how many are coming?"

"Yes, ma'am."

"Won't we need creamer for the coffee?" Mitch wondered, placing a slice of cheese on his bread. "You should probably buy a lot, because I've seen Mr. Delome use a ton!"

"Good idea, Mitch. I've also thought we will purchase some soda. As the morning wears on, it could get pretty warm, and our guests might enjoy a cold soda, although I can't picture Mrs. Bagwell drinking a soda."

"I can hardly wait," Mitch declared.

Max went through the list. "There's eleven coming not including our family. I also didn't add in the Russells' baby."

Mom wrote several things on the paper while Mitch flipped through the sale flyer. "Here's sausage. Isn't Dad grilling sausage, Mom?"

"He is, and that's a reasonable price. I'll write it down. Mollie, you and Mitch should get Mrs. Bagwell's mail and paper right after cleanup so you don't forget."

"Yes, ma'am."

Maddie also wanted to come, so the three set out. They waved at Mr. Delome as they hurried to Mrs. Bagwell's. "We should have brought Maple," Mitch said. "She likes to go for walks."

"It's too hot," Mollie observed. "I saw the temperature was 94!"

"I believe it." Mitch grabbed Mrs. Bagwell's morning paper.

Mollie opened the bag, carefully put the mail in, and folded the paper bag closed. "It would be nice if we had more people who wanted us to do this for them," Mollie said. "Maybe next summer we could hand out flyers."

That afternoon, Mollie helped Grandma for less than their normal amount of time. Grandma had a dentist appointment at three-thirty, and Mollie needed to make cookies for Miss Jenkins. Mom let Maddie take a short nap so that she could help Mollie.

Mollie looked over her Ultimate Chocolate Chip Cookie recipe. "We'll start with creaming part of the ingredients in the mixer. You may help me measure and pour." Mollie grabbed a chair from the dining room and brought it over for Maddie to stand on. "We're buddies, and we're going to work together."

Maddie's face shone with excitement. "Yes! And, I can wear the apron Mommy made me!" She hurried to the pantry

Dish Ultimate Chocolate Chip Cookies   **Yields** 20-22 cookies

3/4 cup Crisco Butter Shortening   2 cups all-purpose flour

1 1/4 cups firmly packed light brown sugar   1 teaspoon salt

2 tablespoons milk   3/4 teaspoon baking soda

1 tablespoon vanilla extract   1 cup semisweet chocolate chips

1 large egg

Heat oven to 375.° Combine Butter Shortening, brown sugar, milk, and vanilla in a large bowl. Beat at medium speed of electric mixer till well blended. Beat in egg. Combine flour, salt, baking soda in a separate bowl and then mix into shortening mixture until just blended. Stir in chocolate chips. Drop dough by spoonfuls onto ungreased cookie sheets. Bake 7-12 minutes until desired doneness. Cool on cookie sheets for 2 minutes before removing to cooling racks. Enjoy!

Note: If you're doubling the cookie recipe, decrease milk by one tablespoon. Also, be cautious not to over beat the batter.

and found the red apron Mom had sewed for her last fall. "It's my favorite one, just like my favorite red jumper that Maple ripped."

"It looks nice," Mollie complimented. She let Maddie pack down each brown sugar cup. Several small lumps of brown sugar found their way into Maddie's mouth.

"I do like sugar," Maddie said, after she had sucked on another brown blob.

Mollie measured the Butter Crisco and scraped it into the bowl. Maddie then put in the specified amount of milk and vanilla. "I'm going to turn the mixer on, so keep your hands back," Mollie warned. "Oh, wait, we forgot to put our hair in ponytails. Let's go do that."

As the girls went upstairs, Maddie asked, "Why do we have to have ponytails?"

"For two reasons. The first is to keep our hair back so it doesn't get accidently caught in the mixer, and the other reason is we don't want a hair to fall into the cookie dough." The girls were soon back, and the mixer whirred on a low speed.

A little after three-thirty, the front door slammed, and the boys came running in. "Ooops!" Mitch covered his mouth. "I hope Moses and Melissa aren't napping."

Mollie glanced at the clock. "They should be up."

"Grandpa wants you to save him a cookie," Max told Mollie. "By the way, when Miss Jenkins was talking to you, did she mention anything about our church services?"

"Yes!" Mollie nodded. "She said the residents are talking about how much they love having church there, and they hope we keep doing it."

"That's neat." Max went to the refrigerator to pour a glass of cold water.

"Max, you know Mr. McGovern, the man who used to be a preacher?"

"Yes, I like him."

"Miss Jenkins said he is really happy now, and it's because of our having church. Maddie," Mollie paused, "you may measure flour and dump it in this bowl. I'll keep track of how many you're putting in. We'll then need to add baking soda and salt."

"I love doing the nursing home service," Max agreed. "Pastor Thompson likes us doing it, too, and he's going to preach at the nursing home next Sunday."

"I didn't know that!" Mitch exclaimed.

"Maddie, you may crack the eggs. We need three." Mollie placed the white eggs on the counter, being careful to not let them roll off. She found a small bowl Maddie could put the eggs into. After the eggs were beaten into the grainy batter, Mollie slowly added the flour mixture.

"I'll put in the chocolate chips when you're ready for that," Max offered.

"Well, I said Maddie could be my helper," Mollie explained to Max. "Maybe why you're offering is so you can eat the chocolate chips."

Max looked sheepish. "You're right; I did want to eat them."

"Everyone can have some," Mollie decided. She portioned out four piles and then turned the mixer off. Mollie scraped the dough from the beaters, placing the bowl near Maddie. "You may measure out three cups of chocolate chips. The dough looks yummy," Mollie declared. "I wish it didn't have uncooked eggs in it so that I'd be able to have a bite." She found baking pans and placed them on the counter. Mitch grabbed two spoons and helped Mollie portion the cookies onto the pans.

"Oh, no!" Mitch realized what time it was. "I'm late for piano practice! Sorry, I have to go."

Mitch was soon pounding out a song Mom had assigned him during their last piano lesson. "You're sounding good," Mollie called. "Maybe you can do a special on Sunday!"

When Mitch was through, the children enjoyed a snack of cookies and milk. After putting more cookies in the oven, they went upstairs to see if they could help Mom with the twins. She had just finished feeding them. "Come in," invited Mom. Her comfortable rocking chair was set in the corner of the room for when she fed the twins.

"May we bring Melissa to our room?" Mollie asked. "I need to organize my drawers."

"It's our reading time. Why don't you get the book from downstairs, and we'll read up here? Then you can organize after that."

"Yes, ma'am!"

"May I hold Moses?" Mitch requested.

"Sure." Mom loved seeing the children take enjoyment from the babies.

"I'd like to hold Melissa then," Max decided.

When Mom had almost finished that afternoon's chapter, Mitch announced: "I smell something burning!"

"Oh, no!" Mollie cried. "Those are my cookies, and I forgot to set a timer!" Mollie raced from the room. Max followed at a slower pace with Melissa, and as he went down the stairs, the strong smell of burned cookies hit him. Mollie was pulling two pans of dark brown blobs from the oven. "That's sad," Mollie moaned.

"I agree," Max said. He observed the pans. "I had been counting on another cookie or two for dessert."

Mom walked in with Moses. "What's a cookie-making afternoon without burning a few? How many more do you need for Miss Jenkins?"

Mollie counted the number of acceptable cookies. "Eight more."

"You have time to make a small batch before dinner."

Mitch contemplated the blobs. "I think they look like chocolate cookies," he noted. "Mom, may I eat the burned ones? They still might be a little good!"

"Yes, but just one so you don't spoil your dinner. We'll save the others for another time."

Promptly at seven, Miss Jenkins showed up. Mom answered the door since Dad was on the phone. "Come in; it's nice to see you."

Mollie hurried to join Mom, and she was surprised to see Miss Jenkins' new hair color: it was dark red, and curled under at her chin. "I can't stay. Work was crazy today, and I've yet to pack for the trip. Oh, wow, she's growing up!" Miss Jenkins patted Melissa's fuzzy hair. "What a cute headband!" Miss Jenkins took the plate of cookies from Mollie. "Thank you! They smell delicious."

"I thought you might enjoy a little treat tonight." Mollie handed Miss Jenkins a sandwich-size plastic bag with two fresh, slightly gooey cookies.

Miss Jenkins seemed pleased, and she gave Mollie a white envelope. "Here's the money. I'll enjoy my cookies—I haven't eaten dinner yet, so this will be it! See you folks later." With that, Miss Jenkins was gone.

"How much did she give you?" Mitch wondered.

"I'm going to see." Mollie tore open the envelope. "Twenty dollars! That's a lot for four dozen cookies. I know what I'll do: save some and give part to Kelia in Africa. Maybe she can buy tracts to give out to people. I heard Dad saying he needs to send in the quarterly support, so I'll give Dad the money to include with his, and I'll write her a letter!" Kelia was the daughter of the national pastor whom the Moodys supported in Africa.

Independence Day was now here. The children rose early, and they were anxious to finish preparations for their neighborhood breakfast. After they had their time in God's Word, they hurried to begin the "to do" list Mom had compiled.

"I'm glad it's not raining!" Mitch observed, as he and Max stepped outside.

"I agree." Max noticed the air felt sticky, but a slight breeze was blowing, which would help the morning not get too hot. Maple bounded after the boys and then raced in circles around the yard. Max tossed a small ball toward the back fence. Rushing after the ball, Maple barely stopped to grab it in her mouth, and she continued to Max, dropping it at his feet. "Good girl. Let's get our card table from the basement."

"Why is it called a card table?" Mitch asked, as they went to retrieve it.

"I don't know; we should ask Dad if we remember." The boys soon had the table set up. "What is next on the list?" Max wondered.

"Chairs," Mitch promptly answered. "Everyone is supposed to bring a lawn chair, but we need some for our family. I'll go see what I can find in the basement, and you can look in the garage."

Several minutes later, Max was coming out of the garage when he heard a noise in the driveway. He looked around the corner to see Grandpa opening the tailgate on his truck. "Hi, Grandpa," Max greeted him. "I didn't know you were here!"

"We arrived a few minutes ago; we had to stop by the bakery for cinnamon rolls. What are you doing?"

"We were trying to find lawn chairs, but I didn't see any in the garage."

"We had a few extra at home, so I stuck them in the truck in case you could use them," Grandpa remarked.

"Thanks, Grandpa. Hopefully Mitch has come up with some too! We should have looked for them earlier."

Mitch hurried around from the backyard. "I found two chairs in the basement."

"Grandpa brought several extra," Max explained.

"Good!"

"How are your preparations coming?" Grandpa asked, sliding a table to the boys from the truck.

"We're getting there. With the storm Saturday afternoon, we couldn't do anything outside. At least it didn't rain a lot."

"I'll take a table, and you boys take another, and then I'll come back for the last." Grandpa picked the table up. "When I was telling your grandma that I was glad you included us in the party, she reminded me that we're practically your neighbors." Grandpa followed the boys to the backyard. "It'll really be a nice morning for a picnic."

After Grandpa retrieved the last table, he joined Dad, who was firing up the barbecue grill. At the same time, preparations inside were moving along. Mitch ran in the back door, letting it slam behind him. "Sorry! How's it going?"

"We're doing well," replied Mollie. "The chocolate chip muffins are done and cooling. Is the backyard ready?"

"Almost; we just put the tablecloths on, and Max is attaching the balloons Dad bought to the tables. We realized we still need all the plates and stuff."

"Maddie and I can get those for you." The girls went to the pantry and collected paper plates, napkins, and eating utensils. They handed them to Mitch who hurried outside. Soon, Mollie and Maddie had the kitchen tidied. "Let's go see how it all looks," Mollie suggested, grabbing the platter of muffins.

"How long 'til people come?" Maddie tugged on Mollie's arm.

"They'll start arriving anytime; I can hardly wait! I need to get the food tag cards and a pen." Mom had thought it would be helpful if each dish brought was labeled so that people would know what it was.

A little later, Mom and Grandma came outside with the twins, who were dressed in patriotic red, white, and blue. Melissa sported a denim jumper while Moses was in overalls. They had on white shirts and red socks. "Wow, they're cute," Mollie exclaimed.

"Each day they just get cuter and cuter, and with them smiling and giggling, it's really sweet." Mom kissed Moses. "We're going to need the stroller."

Mitch overheard Mom's comment and said, "I'll get it!"

Chapter 11

The 4th of July Continued

Mr. Delome and his son, Bill, were the first non-family guests to arrive. "We're glad to have you, Bill," Dad greeted him, shaking his hand.

"Thanks," Bill said. He set down two lawn chairs. "Last time I had breakfast with your family was after the fire. At least it's more pleasant circumstances this time."

Mr. Delome handed a box of donuts to Mollie. "Here are donuts fresh from the Price Slasher bakery."

Mollie popped off her pen lid. "Yummy. What kind are they?"

"Only the best: custard filled and chocolate iced." Mollie thought for a moment, wondering what her description should be. She then wrote *Chocolate frosted and custard filled donuts.* Mitch joined them, and he eyed what Mollie had written. He hoped a donut would be left by the time he went through the line since it had been decided that the Moodys would go through after everyone else.

Mr. Delome spotted the stroller. "Bill, come with me; I want to show you this. A few months ago, I had the privilege of attending my first baby shower. It was for the Moody twins, and this was my gift."

"That's a slick gift you bought them, Dad," Bill approved as he turned to pat Maple, who had snuck up to sniff him. "So, the Moodys had twins? I didn't know that." He peered in the stroller to see the babies. "They're pretty cute babies."

"We love using the stroller," Dad said to Mr. Delome. "Thank you for such a generous gift."

"I'm glad you like it," Mr. Delome returned. "Wow. You did up these tables so nicely, I feel like I'm at an important party!" The food tables had been decorated in a 4th of July theme. Dad and the children had gone shopping at the craft store to purchase tablecloths and a few other items. The children had made a "Happy 4th of July" banner by printing out large letters from the computer, using white and red paper. A bunch of patriotic colored balloons decorated the ends of the tables.

"Hello!" Mrs. Bagwell bustled into the backyard with a large pan in her hand. "Where should I put the food? I brought a lot, because I know Mix and Match eat a bunch. Oliver, what'd you bring?" she asked without waiting for an answer to her first question.

"Donuts."

"Not surprising." Mrs. Bagwell shook her head. "I wouldn't have expected you to cook up something."

Mr. Delome chuckled. "I do plan to start learning how to cook and bake. As a matter of fact, it's on my rather lengthy list of things I want to learn. Mollie needs to know what you brought."

"Why?"

"Because she's writing it down so we'll know what we're going to partake of."

Mrs. Bagwell smiled. "It's an egg and cheese breakfast casserole. Who is that fellow with you?"

"My son, Bill. Bill, this is Maud Bagwell, and Maud, this is Bill. He came for a visit."

Bill shook Mrs. Bagwell's hand. "Nice to meet you."

"Now," Mr. Delome looked around, "I want to see these prize sunflowers you have been telling me about. I may have to ask Grandma Moody for seeds of my own!" Max took Mr. Delome to the area where the sunflowers were and showed him. "They're very tall already," Mr. Delome observed. "I can see where the heads will be blossoming soon. Hmmmm … I may have to try my hand at gardening."

A bark was heard, and they turned to see Honey, Grandma Clifton's dog, tugging at the leash Grandma Clifton was holding. "I'm glad you brought Honey," Max remarked. "Dad said we could try Maple being off leash unless she is too wild or knocks people's drinks over."

Grandma Clifton handed a pan to Max. "I brought coffee cake."

"I can smell it," Max declared, taking the pan from her.

*"Wow. You did up these tables so nicely,
I feel like I'm at an important party!"*

Soon, the Russells came, and Mrs. Russell was pushing Madison in a stroller. Mr. Russell, a tall man, carried a good-sized pot. When they reached the small group at the food table, Mr. Delome tapped the pot: "What do you have in there?—Mollie needs to know."

"Sausage gravy, and the biscuits are in the stroller. I made a fair bit, because Maud thinks the Moody boys eat a lot!"

A young family arrived, and it was the man they had caroled to last winter whose mother had died. The man was dressed simply in jeans and a polo shirt, and he wore a pair of reflective sunglasses. His wife's blond hair was pinned up in a clip, and she was obviously expecting a baby. A little girl toddled next to the wife. Dad hurried over to them. "Welcome, Alex! I know we caroled to you, but your wife and daughter weren't there, and I'm afraid I don't know their names or even your last name. I'm Jim Moody."

"Thanks for inviting us; we've been looking forward to it. We're the Wrights, and this is my wife, Ellie," Alex replied. "This is Chloe, and we also have a boy on the way," he added. "Thank you for taking the time to carol. Christmas was pretty rough with losing my mom, whom Ellie had been caring for. But, we're doing fine now." Alex was holding two lawn chairs.

"Losing a loved one is always hard," Dad sympathized as Ellie gave a stainless steel bowl covered with foil to Mitch.

"Mrs. Wright," Mitch began, "would you mind telling us what you brought? My sister is writing food tags so people will know what is what."

"We brought a fruit salad." Mitch wondered to himself why a person would eat a salad for breakfast, but he decided he would wait to form an opinion until he tried the dish.

"I think we'll go ahead and start," Dad announced. "I'll begin with blessing the food."

Mr. Delome poked Bill. "The hat," Mr. Delome whispered, and Bill looked bewildered for a brief moment, but then he quickly recovered.

"I forgot," Bill whispered back, hastily removing his hat.

"Dear Heavenly Father, thank You for this Independence Day, a day we celebrate our country's freedom. Most importantly, thank You for sending Your Son, Jesus, to die on the cross for our sins and to pay our penalty. May we never take that incredible sacrifice for granted. Please bless this food, which many hands have prepared. In Jesus' Name, Amen. Okay," Dad continued. "We've set up breakfast buffet style. Mollie made food tags for each dish so you will know what it is. We also have three different kinds of sausage. For drinks, we have water, coffee, soda, and Rosie's juice. Rosie's juice is a mixture of orange and cranberry juice. Please start in!"

Soon, the buffet line was formed, and their guests seemed to enjoy the variety of breakfast foods. Mollie and Mitch stood at the end of the second table, filling drinks. Finally, all the Moodys' guests had gone through the buffet line and found comfortable places to sit. As Mitch worked through the food table, he was glad to see some donuts left, and he also decided to try the fruit salad.

Grandma Clifton chose a spot in the shade, and Honey lay obediently next to her. "May we join you?" Grandma asked Grandma Clifton, as she and Mrs. Bagwell walked toward her.

"Please do."

"The children have told me about you," Grandma remarked to Mrs. Bagwell, "but we've never really talked. I'd love to know about yourself and your family."

Mrs. Bagwell shrugged her shoulders. "I don't know if I have a lot to tell, but if you ladies want to hear it—"

Grandma looked at Grandma Clifton. "I'm assuming you'd like to?"

"Oh, yes. I'd love to hear."

"Okay, but does that sausage looks delicious," Mrs. Bagwell commented to Grandma Clifton.

"I'll get you a piece," offered Grandma Clifton.

"No thanks; I was just thinking how wonderful it would taste. My stomach has been bothering me lately, so I'm avoiding greasy food. Well, I was raised by my grandparents . . ."

In the meantime, Mr. and Mrs. Russell were chatting with Grandpa, and Dad was talking with Mr. Wright, Mr. Delome, and Bill. Max saw Madison, the Russells' baby who was a few weeks older than the twins, squirming and grabbing for Mrs. Russell's plate. "May I hold Madison for you?" Max offered.

"Sure! He's learning to reach for things, and he seems to want whatever I have, so watch your plate. Thank you!" Mrs. Russell handed Madison to Max.

Max sat on a chair next to Grandpa and listened to the conversation. Mrs. Russell excused herself and headed for Mom, who was talking with Mrs. Wright. Occasionally, Grandpa would try to get Madison to smile by making a face. "So," Mr. Russell addressed Grandpa, "you'll be living right next door to Jim, Emily, and their children?"

"Yep. We're hoping to move sometime in August. We're doing projects on the house that would be hard to do once we are living in it. Plus we have all the packing and cleaning at the other house to get done."

Mr. Russell nodded. "I sure hope it works out for you. I really can't imagine moving near my parents or Kim's either."

"We have a good relationship with Jim and Emily, and we think living close will make it that much better. We have lived about eleven minutes away for ten months now, and that has been going so well that we were all in favor of buying the house next door to them when it came up for sale. Ask me in six months how it has been going, and I hope I have a good report to give you. Tell me, Dave, do you go to church?"

"Only to make Kim happy. I am not much into religion myself, but Kim seems to like it. I find a reason to stay home more often than I go. Where do you work?" Mr. Russell changed the subject.

Over in the shade, Mollie and Maddie sat quietly near Mom. Mollie now held Moses, while Mom was holding Melissa. Chloe, the Wright's little girl, walked over to Mollie. "Hi," she said, grinning at Mollie.

"You must be Chloe; I'm Mollie. How old are you?" Mollie asked. Chloe held up two fingers. "Two! Wow! You're becoming a big girl. Did you already eat breakfast?"

Chloe nodded. "I ate before we comed here. I like that baby." She gently ran her hand over Moses' arm.

A movement near the back door caught Mollie's attention. Maple lay in the grass, and it seemed she had something in her mouth. Maddie also had noticed, and she ran over to Maple. "Mollie," she called. "Come here. Maple's eating something."

Mollie waited for a pause in Mom's conversation to tell her that she was going to put Moses back in the stroller. After she had buckled Moses into the stroller, Mollie turned to Chloe. "Would you like to come with me?" Without answering,

Chloe shyly took Mollie's hand. They hurried over to where Maple was. A small piece of crinkly-looking white paper peeked from her mouth. "Maple, drop it." Maple's ears hung flat, but she kept her jaw tightly shut. Mollie tapped her muzzle. "Drop it, Maple."

"It's not working," a voice matter-of-factly stated. Mollie whirled around and saw Bill watching them. He grinned. "I can help you, because I carry dog treats for my dog." Bill knelt on the grass next to Maple, and Maple seemed slightly nervous. She clenched the object tighter and looked as if she would get up.

"Maple," Bill spoke quietly. "Drop it." Maple slowly sat up and sniffed Bill's hand. She kept her jaw resolutely shut. "Here," Bill handed the treat to Maddie. "Maybe she'll take it from you."

"Drop it," Maddie instructed to Maple, and Maple quickly dropped her treasure. "Good girl!" Maddie praised her, while Maple crunched on the treat.

"What is it?" Mitch joined the group with Honey on leash. Honey sniffed Bill's hand disappointedly.

"Great. Now *she's* wanting a treat," Bill laughed. At the word "treat," Honey's ears perked up. "She even knows what that means! Okay." He dug a little deeper into his pocket. "I have another one." Bill gave it to her. "She's a fine-looking golden. So what was Maple eating?"

"A muffin liner," Mollie told him.

Meanwhile, Mrs. Russell, Mrs. Wright, and Mom were having a pleasant conversation. Mrs. Russell looked at Mom. "Ellie already knows this, but I've been waiting for an opportunity to tell you. We found out we're expecting again. I told Dave that I'm hoping for a girl."

"That's wonderful," Mom congratulated her.

Mrs. Wright nodded. "Since we live close, I told Kim it'd be nice for our babies to be playmates."

"Besides that, I have some more news," Mrs. Russell continued. "I've decided not to teach school anymore, and instead, I'll be a stay-at-home mom. Dave's happy, and I'm happy, although a little nervous."

Mom's face lit up. "Oh, Kim, I think you will like being home with Madison and your new baby full time. No more trying to juggle a job, children, and home. You could put your teaching skills to work with your own children. Other people can teach and do what you do at school, but you're the only mommy who can raise your children. I'm so excited for you!"

The neighbors lingered for quite a while, enjoying each other's company, until late morning when they began going home. Grandpa and Grandma stayed to help with the cleanup. "I certainly liked your 4th of July breakfast picnic. What an opportunity to meet and get to know our new neighbors," Grandma exclaimed, as she came in the house with an armload of things.

"And," Mitch told Grandpa, "I've decided I like fruit salad."

Chapter 12

A Clean Van

Another Saturday had arrived, and an idea was on Mitch's mind when he woke up. "Max, I think we should wash the van and clean the inside as a surprise for Mom."

"How would that surprise her when she could look out the window and see us?" Max lowered his voice to a whisper, remembering Moses was still asleep.

"I heard that Mom and Grandma might go shopping this morning, and we can do it while they're away."

"Let's try for it," Max agreed. The boys slipped from the room to have their Bible time in the living room.

"Dad's not here; he must have gotten up early and already had his time with the Lord," Mitch commented. "I always like it when he's here with us. Oh, well."

Mollie joined them with her Bible, and Mitch told her his idea. "I like that, Mitch," she remarked. Maddie trotted in, found the CD player, and snuggled next to Mollie to listen to the Bible.

A little later, Dad and Mom came down with the twins. "Good morning!" Dad greeted them. Mom had Melissa in the sling, and she stepped into the kitchen to begin breakfast.

Mitch hurried to Dad, whispering, "I want to ask you something." Dad leaned toward Mitch. "I'd like to know if we may wash and clean the van as a surprise for Mom if she goes shopping."

"Sure! I'll pull the van from the garage after she leaves!"

At breakfast, Mom explained that she and Grandma had decided to go shopping. "Grandma wanted company, and Dad thought it'd be nice for me to have an outing. We'll be back right after lunch."

"When are you leaving?" Mollie wondered.

"I'll feed the twins after breakfast, and then we'll go."

When Grandma came, Dad helped her buckle the twins' car seats in her car. The children could hardly wait for Mom and the twins to leave! Grandma's car was soon out of sight, and Dad backed the van from the garage. "Mom is going to be very happy," Dad encouraged them. "I'll be inside trying to catch up on some bank paperwork I let go while we had that big work project."

Mitch grabbed a bucket, and Max uncoiled the hose. "Where's the nozzle?" Max walked around the area where it should have been. "Someone didn't put it away where it belongs," he complained.

"I know where it is," Mollie offered. "I used it in the back-yard for my sunflowers since they need more than a watering can's worth of water now."

"Dad says we always should keep the nozzle right here," Max fussed at Mollie. "I'll go ahead and start washing the van without it, but please hurry and get it."

"I'm sorry, Max," Mollie apologized.

Max placed his thumb over the hose opening and used his thumb like a nozzle. Water vigorously shot out around the edges and began to soak him. "This isn't a good solution," Max grumbled.

A few minutes later, Mollie returned with the nozzle. "Here you go, Max."

"Thanks, Mollie. While you were gone, the Lord convicted me of my anger. Please forgive me. I don't put things away where they belong all the time either." Max took the brass nozzle, struggling to twist it on. Water sprayed in every direction, and if he thought he was wet before, he was really wet now!

"I'll turn the water off." Mitch ran for the water spigot.

Just then, Mr. Delome hurried across the street. "When you're through, you can give my car a bath!" he exclaimed with a smile.

"We're surprising Mom by cleaning the van," Mitch informed him, waiting near the water spigot for Max to screw the nozzle on.

"I'm sure your mom will be blessed." Mr. Delome watched Max. "You're pretty wet."

"We couldn't find the nozzle to start with, so I made the mistake of trying to use my thumb as a nozzle. Then I was too lazy to go turn the water off. Okay, Mitch," Max called. "You may turn it back on. Maddie, I'll let you spray the van." Max walked around the van with her, demonstrating how to do it.

Mitch dipped a sponge into the sudsy water and scrubbed the front of the van. Mr. Delome observed Mitch. "Smashed, dried bugs are tough to get off, aren't they?"

"They sure are."

"Bill left yesterday," Mr. Delome informed them. "And I'm feeling lonely already. It was wonderful having another person around. We had our best visit ever because we didn't argue. In the past, we never shouted over things, but we could get pretty unhappy with each other. This was our first visit since I've been saved, and when Bill would say something I would normally get mad about, I just prayed the Lord would help me not to say things I shouldn't. Every morning, I woke up early to have my time with the Lord, and I have even been memorizing Scripture about not being angry, which helped. Bill also came to church, and he liked Pastor Thompson's message."

"Were you able to witness to him?" Mollie vigorously rubbed on a black streak on the side of the van. "It looks like we drove through tar."

"Let me try." Mr. Delome took Mollie's sponge and instructed Maddie, "Spray this area."

Maddie obediently followed Mr. Delome's instructions. "To answer your question, I did share the Lord with him. He wasn't too interested, yet he listened. He wasn't awake when I would read the Bible in the morning, but in the evenings, he would listen when I read a chapter of Scripture. Max, you've missed several spots over here." Mr. Delome pointed to a small section, and Max used his sponge to clean the area.

"Speaking of witnessing, we're praying for Mrs. Bagwell's salvation," Max said. "She never talks about the Lord, and we as a family are praying for her and opportunities to share Jesus."

"I'm praying too," Mr. Delome agreed, "and I've also been trying to witness to her. I don't know if I'm doing a whole lot of good, but I'm working on it. Maud's pretty set in her ways and self-sufficient. But, I figure I have to learn how to witness by trial and error."

Mitch went to the house to turn down the water pressure. He then asked Maddie, "May I borrow the hose?"

"Sure." Maddie obligingly handed it to Mitch, curious what he had in mind.

Mitch called, "Maple, come here!" The dog lazily lifted her head from her spot in the yard. "Do you want a drink?" Mitch held the hose out while Maple trotted over. Maple happily lapped from the stream of water.

Mr. Delome and the children continued to chat until the van was clean. "I'll inspect now," Mr. Delome offered. "Here's a spot, and another one over here, and one on this side," he nodded. "When that's taken care of, you're ready to dry it."

Maple happily lapped from the stream of water.

"Thanks for your help," Max said, as he worked on the areas Mr. Delome had pointed out. "Maddie, you may do a final rinse."

Mitch found the special absorbent rag they used to dry the van and car after they had been washed. If the van air-dried, there would be noticeable water spots. "Max, I'll dry the van if you want to vacuum," Mitch decided.

"Thanks," Max agreed. "Mollie, why don't you clean the windows, and Maddie you may pick up the trash."

Mr. Delome emptied the bucket of dirty water in the street, and after turning the water off, he coiled up the hose. Soon, the van was clean, and Max went inside to ask Dad to come see their finished product. Dad came outside and greeted Mr. Delome.

"Howdy, Jim!" Mr. Delome replied.

"Wow, the van looks beautiful!" Dad saw the silver twelve-passenger van sparkle in the sunlight. He opened a door. "You cleaned the inside too, I think! I could do the white glove test, and it would still be white!" The four children beamed at Dad's compliment.

"I'm glad," Mitch said. "I can't wait for Mom to see it!"

"She'll be happy." Dad glanced at his watch. "We need to run to the store to pick up a few things."

"All right, I'll be seeing you later!" Mr. Delome waved and headed across the street.

Dad decided to take his car, since he didn't want to mess up the nice work on the van. When they arrived at the grocery store, Dad said, "I don't think we need a cart. Max and Mitch, you may go together and find a gallon of two percent milk, the Big Save brand, and two dozen eggs. The girls and I will get salt and bread." Dad held his girls' hands as they strolled through the store to the baking aisle. "Mom said we're almost out of salt, so we'll grab a package." They located the small box and went to the bread section. The coffee-bean grinding area was directly across from the bread.

"Yumm." Mollie breathed deeply of the fragrant aroma. "I love the way that coffee smells. Do you like coffee, Dad?"

"Yes, but I only drink a cup now and then, like on holidays or when we're with Grandpa and Grandma. Let's see." Dad turned to the bread and evaluated the choices. "We'll get three of these."

Mollie saw the price was marked ninety-nine cents. "Why are we getting white bread? Usually we eat our homemade whole wheat bread."

"I guess you'll have to wait and see." Mollie saw the twinkle in Dad's eyes. They rounded the corner and almost bumped into Dad's coworker, Anthony Johnson, and his little boy, Joe. "Anthony, it's great to see you!"

"You too, Moody. Running a few errands?" Mr. Johnson asked.

"Yes, we are. Wow, Joe, you've grown up since we saw you last winter," Dad remarked.

The blond-haired boy spotted an end-aisle display of cookies. Joe grabbed a package and shook it vigorously. "I want this!" he begged Mr. Johnson. "I'm hungry!"

Mr. Johnson laughed. "We'll get them, but you need to wait until after lunch to eat them." Joe stood quietly next to his dad. He flipped the package over as if he were reading the ingredient list. Mr. Johnson turned to Dad. "Did you make your project deadline yesterday? I didn't get a chance to stop over in your area."

"Yes, we did. Now I'm working to catch up on the regular things I let slide while I was involved in the project."

Joe walked over to Maddie and said, "My name is Joe; what's yours?"

"Madelyn Moody," she announced. "But you can call me Maddie."

Joe went to Mollie. "My name is Joe; what's yours?"

"Mollie."

"Good job, Joe," Mr. Johnson encouraged. "We're working with him on some manners, and I'd say we've made progress. Well, we'd better be going, or Mom will wonder what happened to us. Nice to see you all!"

Max and Mitch joined Dad and the girls. "We had trouble finding eggs that weren't cracked," Max reported. "Mitch probably went through fifty dozen looking for the two that were okay."

"Fifty dozen?" Dad questioned.

"Well, Max was probably exaggerating, but it seemed like it!" Mitch agreed.

After they checked out and were in the car, Mollie told the boys about Mr. Johnson and Joe. "Joe has become more obedient since last time; have you been talking to him, Dad?"

"It comes up in our conversation every now and then. I guess Mr. and Mrs. Johnson have been working hard with Joe; he's much different than the last time we were around him!" The light turned yellow, and Dad stopped. "What's going on over there?" Dad wondered.

"I see a bulldozer." Mitch shielded his eyes from the sun. "Someone is tearing down that house."

A small, thin man was in the street, waving people from the right lane and pointing them to move into the left. Cars honked unhappily as people switched lanes. "I know who that is!" Max declared. "It's Mr. Coppen's worker-guy, Joe. I imagine—yes, I do see Mr. Coppen in the bulldozer."

"The house was pretty dilapidated." Mitch looked at the demolition as they drove by.

Dad pulled into a fast-food parking lot. "Mom and Grandma were going out for lunch, so I've decided we'll stop for something. Everyone may pick two items off the value menu, and then you may have an ice cream cone for dessert!"

The children thoroughly enjoyed their lunch, and a little later, they headed home. As they drove down Strawberry Lane, Max said, "Grandma and Mom must be home; Grandma's car is in the driveway!"

They all went inside and found Grandma and Mom talking in the living room. Mom's face sparkled, and they knew she had seen the van. "I noticed the clean van right away! Grandma suggested I look inside, and I was doubly delighted that it was vacuumed and the windows cleaned. Thank you!" Mom went to each child and gave them all a kiss.

Chapter

13

Family Night

It was now Friday, July 15th, and Dad announced a Family Night that evening. "What are we going to do?" Mitch wondered.

"Well," Dad began, "we'll eat dinner a little early and then have Bible time. After that, Mom will feed the twins, and we'll head out."

"Head out?" Max repeated.

"Yes, head out," Dad grinned. "Oh, and tonight is a memory verse review. I forgot last week. I'd better be off to work." He kissed Mom and hurried to the garage.

Late that afternoon, the children were reviewing their Scripture memory verses. Max comfortably lay on his back, eyes closed and mouth moving. Mollie sat on the couch, diligently working, and Mitch was near the front window. Mitch sighed. "Someone's dogs are barking. I think they've barked at least a hundred times in the last five minutes, and it's driving me crazy: I can hardly concentrate on my verses."

"I know, but you need to be working on them," Max said. "I'm hoping to have mine ready by the time Dad gets home."

"You're right." Mitch slid away from the window to help himself not be distracted. A few minutes later, Mitch raised himself up on an elbow: "Mollie, do you think you should put the pizza dough on pans?"

"It has probably risen enough." Mollie hopped up.

After she left, Mitch said, "No one has brought the mail in. I'm going to get it." He was delighted to find two cards among other mail items. "Max!" he exclaimed, rushing in the door. "We received a card from the Russells and another from the Wrights. I imagine they're 'thank you' notes for the picnic! I can't wait until we can open them."

A little later, Mollie rejoined the boys in the living room, and Mitch showed her his prize notes. "I really liked what we did on the 4th of July," Mollie said. "Hopefully we can do it every year! Max, will you please listen to my verses? I'm in First Peter, one."

"Sure."

"First Peter, chapter one. Peter, an apostle of Jesus Christ, to the strangers scattered throughout Pontus, Galatia, Cappadocia, Asia, and Bithynia. . ."

Maple perked her ears at the sound of the garage door and began barking. "Quiet, Maple! It's just Dad." Mitch patted the golden retriever.

Soon, Dad came in the house, and Maple bounded for him. "Nice to see you too!" He scratched her ears. "It delights my heart to see you children with your Bibles out: you must be working on Scripture memory!"

"Yes," Max nodded. "Mine are ready."

"I'll listen to them before dinner. Are we on schedule for an early dinner?"

"Yes. I put the pizza dough out," Mollie answered, "and Max is going to do the rest."

"Dad!" Mitch had been waiting for an opportunity to say something. "We received two cards in the mail today! May I open them now?"

"Okay; read them aloud to us."

Mitch tore open the first note and read: "Dear Moody Family, Thank you for the delightful breakfast picnic on the 4th. Dave and I really enjoyed getting to know our neighbors more. Madison enjoyed his time with Max, and I liked having a break! Count us in if you want to do it next year. The food was also delicious! Sincerely, Kim, Dave, and Madison." He opened the next one and said, "Now this is from the Wrights. 'Hi Moodys, Ella, Chloe, and I had a blast at your picnic. The food was excellent, but the chatting was even more enjoyable. Chloe liked being with your oldest daughter. Thank you for showing an interest in Chloe. We'll be trying to return your hospitality with dinner some night over here. Thanks again. Regards, The Wrights.'"

"Those are nice cards. I'll take them to Mom, and we'll be down soon."

Max finished listening to Mollie's verses, and then he went to the kitchen. He preheated the oven to 450 degrees before sliding in the pizza crusts to pre-bake. He stirred the sauce mixture, which consisted of cooked hamburger meat and two cans of pizza sauce. *Smells delicious,* he thought to himself. Ten minutes later, he pulled the crusts from the oven and spread sauce on each crust. He then sprinkled handfuls of mozzarella cheese over it and layered pepperoni on top.

After dinner, Dad said, "Let's move on to Bible time, and then we'll clean up while Mom feeds the twins."

When Bible time was finished, Mom went to take care of the twins while the rest worked on cleanup. "We made a big mess," Max observed, looking at the pile of dishes.

"It was worth it," Mollie responded. "That pizza was yummy!" A while later, Mom called down and said she could use someone to help her get the twins ready.

"What should we wear?" Mitch asked Dad, who was starting up the stairs to help Mom.

Dad glanced at Mitch's clothes. "What you have on will be fine, but wear your walking shoes."

"I know where my shoes are," Maddie announced, skipping into her room where Mom was changing Melissa. "I put them where they go, like you told me."

"Good job," Mom praised her. "Now you won't have to run around looking for them."

Ten minutes later, the family was ready. Dad and Max carried the twins to the van, and Dad buckled them in. "Emily, I almost forgot our supplies. Would you please get them?"

"I'll be happy to." Mom hoped the bread wasn't still in the freezer. She couldn't remember if she had put it in the pantry to defrost. She was relieved to find it defrosted, so she grabbed the loaves, and quietly slid them into the back of the van.

No one asked questions as Mom climbed in the van, and Max closed her door. Dad and Mom enjoyed talking to each other on the drive, while the children silently watched the turns Dad made, but they still couldn't decide where Dad was taking them. "We're kind of going the way to Dad's work but it's not quite right," Mitch remarked. The next turn was definitely not on any normal route.

Five minutes later, Dad pulled into a large parking lot, and the mystery was over: they were at Mayfield's Park. Mayfield's had a nice pond for fishing, a few walking trails, and a small playground. "We're here," Dad announced as he shut off the engine. "We're going to feed the ducks!"

"Oh, really!" Mitch exclaimed. "This'll be great."

"I agree," Max said.

After everyone unloaded, Dad grabbed the white bread from the back of the van. He took the stroller, and they walked toward the pond, where a large group of ducks was clustered. "Children," Dad instructed, "be careful to stay a safe distance back from the water. Maddie, you need to stay close to Mom or me."

Several ducks pecked at the ground. "They are hungry," Maddie observed. "I'm just goin' to watch thems."

"May we get into the bread, please, Dad?" Mitch requested.

"Yes." Dad handed a loaf to Mitch.

After Max, Mollie, and Mitch grabbed several pieces of the white, almost doughy bread, Mitch put the bread in the bottom of the stroller, and the children slowly approached the ducks. *Quack, quack, quack.* Two ducks waddled straight for Mitch. He tore off a few pieces and threw them. One duck caught a piece in mid-air. Mollie saw a tall, stately looking duck. "Look, Dad, how big this one is," Mollie observed.

"It's actually a Canada goose," Dad explained. "There are several in with the ducks." Mollie cast a small portion of the bread to the goose, and it was quickly eaten.

Maddie tugged on Dad's shirt. "May I please feed that duck now?" she asked, pointing to another large goose.

"Sure."

Maddie reached into the bag and selected one piece of bread. Maddie walked slowly toward the goose, step by step, softly calling, "Here, Duckee, Duckee. Here, Duckee, Duckee." Suddenly, the goose began a swift waddle toward Maddie. Horrified, she threw the piece in the greedy goose's direction and ran to Dad. "It's going to get me!" Maddie clung to Dad's legs.

Dad laughed. "No, he was coming for the bread you had. See? Look at him eat." Dad pulled several more pieces of bread from the bag he carried and took Maddie by the hand. "Let's try again." Maddie clutched Dad's hand as they approached the goose.

"I'm going to show you how to do it." Dad broke off chunks and threw them toward the goose. "If you do it this way, he won't try to eat it from your hand. That's when he could accidently bite, so you need to throw it."

Maddie followed Dad's instructions, and her timidity melted away. The black-necked goose pecked at the bread on the ground. Mom shielded her eyes from the sun, watching her family enjoy the ducks. *Thank You, Lord Jesus,* she silently prayed, *for a wonderful family.* A fuss from Moses made her look down at him. "Moses, do you see the ducks?" He began crying, and Mom glanced at Melissa, who had been asleep, but her eyes popped open. "This could be interesting," Mom said aloud.

"Mollie!" Mitch called, laughing. "Help me! Please get more bread, and make it quick! I'm trapped by hungry ducks!"

Mollie glanced toward Mitch. A large group of ducks surrounded him, quacking and making noise. His last piece of bread was fast disappearing. Mollie left the duck she had been feeding and ran for Mom. "May I have the bread?" she asked breathlessly. "Mitch needs it!"

Suddenly, the goose began a swift waddle toward Maddie. Horrified, she threw the piece in the greedy goose's direction and ran to Dad.

Mom handed a loaf to Mollie. "Take the whole thing."

"Thanks, Mom!" Mollie dashed toward Mitch.

"Stay back, stay back, wherever you are!" Mitch hopped up and down, talking to the ducks. "Better hurry, Mollie. I don't think they like being hungry after they've tasted that bread!"

Dad amusedly watched the situation. Mollie threw several pieces of bread toward Mitch, but the breeze blew them slightly off course, and Mitch only caught one. The ducks dove for the other pieces and made short work of them. Mollie stepped closer, giving him more bread. "Thanks, Mollie."

Fifteen minutes passed, and the bread was gone. "Since we've used up the bread, we'll take a walk around the pond," Dad suggested.

Max watched a group of ducks waddle toward the water. "Dad, thanks for bringing us here. I really enjoyed being able to feed the ducks. They are very interesting to watch."

"You're welcome. I was trying to think of something different to do for Family Night. In another month or two, we're going to have either the Russells or the Wrights to dinner as our Family Night."

"I like that!" Mitch said. "May I push the stroller?"

"Yes."

Dad took Mom's hand, and they started off on the small loop next to the pond. A goose hurried after Max, quacking loudly. He laughed. "Sorry, no more bread!"

Ten minutes later, the walk was done, and it was time to leave. Talk filled the van about their duck-feeding experience. Suddenly, Mitch poked Max. "We're not going home the usual way."

"Maybe we have to stop by the grocery store for something."

At the next intersection, Dad turned his blinker on, and Mitch whispered to Max, "There's only one place down here that we go!"

Mollie leaned back. "Do you think we're going where I'm thinking?"

"Sure do!" Mitch's smile was huge.

"Anyone hungry for ice cream?" Dad glanced in the rear view mirror and saw four eager faces. "I thought so. At the beginning of the school year, Mom said if you kept all your tests in order, and didn't lose any so we could use them for the next child, you would get ice cream as a reward. She told me recently that you all passed!"

"Thank you, Dad!" Max expressed his gratefulness.

Dad found a parking spot. "Be thinking about what you want to order as we go in. We'll order in two groups, because I know they have a tendency to make mistakes on our order if we have one large group. Max, Mollie, and Mitch will be in one, and Mom, Maddie, and I in the other."

"Sounds like a good plan," Mom agreed.

"Emily, do you want to use the stroller?"

"I don't think so. I'll put Melissa in the sling, and maybe you could hold Moses."

They walked into the brightly lit store, and the grinding whir of the blizzard machine and the aroma of French fries greeted them. "May I take your order?" A thin girl with a blond-streaked ponytail drummed her fingers on the counter.

"I'd like an M&M blizzard," Mitch said.

"What size?"

"Medium, please."

"I'll take a medium Oreo blizzard." Max paused. "Or, do I want M&M? No, I'll stay with Oreo."

"For you, Sweetie?" The girl looked at Mollie.

"I'd like a small cookie dough blizzard."

The girl tapped the computer screen in several places. "What about for the others?"

"We're going to split our order to make things simpler," Dad explained.

The girl laughed. "You don't need to; I can handle it."

"It's easier this way."

"Okay." After Dad, Mom, and Maddie ordered, they joined Max, Mollie, and Mitch who had scooted two tables together for the family.

"Mitch and I will get the drinks and wait for our orders," Max offered.

Mitch filled each cup with ice and water. "I guess we'll need a tray," Mitch decided. Just then, their first order number was called.

Max picked up the tray and went over to Mitch. "There's room for several drinks here, and we can put the rest on the other tray." Max found the napkins and added them to the tray.

"Order 346."

"I'll get it, Mitch." Max left the first tray with Mitch.

Max handed out the treats while Mitch dispersed the water. "I think we'll pray. Even though it's not a normal meal, we still want to thank the Lord for it," Dad suggested. The family was soon enjoying their delicious ice cream treats. Melissa was fast asleep in the sling, but Moses was awake. "I haven't had a sundae for a long time!" Dad put another spoonful in his mouth.

"Watch out, Dad!" Mitch exclaimed as Maddie reached for a napkin. A cascade of ice-cold water from Maddie's cup poured into Dad's lap and onto Moses. The freezing water shocked both of them. It only took a few seconds before Moses began crying. Mom grabbed a spit-up rag from the diaper bag and handed it over to Dad, who vainly tried to dry the baby off.

"I'm so sorry!" Maddie dabbed at Moses with a napkin. "I didn't mean to spill my drink."

"That's okay," Dad smiled. "Emily, do you have a change of pants for Moses? It mainly seems to be his pants that are wet."

"I do," Mom answered, and she handed the diaper bag to Dad.

"Good; at least this was our last stop."

Soon, the spill had been mopped up as much as possible, and everyone finished their ice cream treats. "Thank you for the ice cream, Daddy," Maddie said. Her mouth had a white tinge around it. "It was yummy."

"You're welcome."

Chapter 14

Dinner with Mrs. Bagwell

It was a sticky, hot Saturday afternoon, and the Moodys were doing projects inside. Dad took several bags of buns from the freezer and turned to Mom, who was opening packages of ground beef for hamburgers. "It's late notice, but I think we should have someone over for dinner. I felt the Lord prompted me that we should invite Mrs. Bagwell. What do you think?"

Mom nodded. "We've never had her over for a meal, and I imagine she'd enjoy it."

Dad found Mrs. Bagwell's number in the phone book, and after he made the call, he was smiling. "She said she'd come. I told her we'll eat around 5:30, and she could come a little earlier if she'd like."

Mom pulled several pieces of bread from the toaster. The Moodys had found it more economical to make their own bread crumbs using toasted bread and blending it to fine crumbs rather than using store-bought bread crumbs. Mom also chopped an onion and then blended it to small pieces. Dad cracked two eggs in a separate bowl and dumped them into the mixture of meat, bread crumbs, and onion. He added salt and pepper as seasoning and then vigorously mixed the ingredients. Max helped shape patties, and he and Dad layered the hamburgers, using wax paper between each layer, in a pan to be carried to the barbecue.

Around five o'clock, the meat was cooking on the grill while the Moodys were talking in the living room. The twins were on a blanket, and the whole family was gathered near them. Mitch dug Aunt Olga's play telephone from the toy tub and pushed buttons. Melissa watched Mitch with interest and made little "ihh ihh" noises. "You want it now, do you?" Mitch asked. "Come over here." Mitch patted the carpet. "You can do it."

"She's not rolled from her tummy to her back," Mom said. "But she's getting close. I don't think you can coax her into it yet."

Mitch grinned. "I'll try. Come on, Melissa! You can do it!" Melissa's brown eyes were fastened on Mitch, and she reached for him. "Uhhhh, uhhhh!" Melissa cooed, her small arm stretching as far as she could and suddenly she flipped over.

"You did it!" Mom laughed.

Mitch held the toy out to Melissa. "Good girl—you rolled over!"

Melissa happily sucked on the phone; Moses fussed, as if he realized Melissa could do something he couldn't. "You're not quite there, are you?" Mom tickled him.

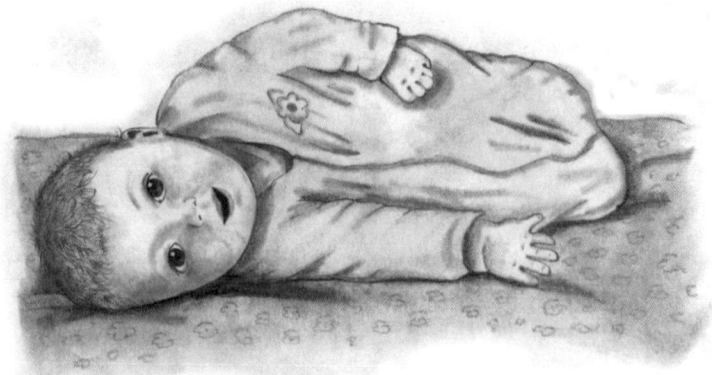

Mitch grinned. "I'll try. Come on, Melissa! You can do it!"

The doorbell rang, and Dad welcomed Mrs. Bagwell. "It looks like I'm interrupting something important," she remarked, handing a small bouquet of flowers to Mom.

"Thank you! The flowers are very pretty. We are excited because Melissa just rolled from her tummy to her back!"

"Those little things are really important when they are young." Mrs. Bagwell sank down on the couch. "This hot weather is draining me lately."

"Does your air conditioner work?" Dad wondered.

"Of course, but it's too expensive to keep it as cool as a body wants."

Soon, the family gathered at the table with their guest. Mom set a pot of baked beans near Dad. "This all looks scrumptious," Mrs. Bagwell observed, sitting next to Mitch. "I've not had a big appetite lately, but this should be wonderful." She looked around expectantly. "I'm sorry; I'm talking too much."

"Go right ahead. We don't mind," Dad said. "We normally pray before we eat."

"I forgot you say grace before you ate; the children did that last winter when they were visiting at my house, and we had cookies. I'll be quiet."

"What's grace?" Maddie piped in.

"It's another word for praying." Dad paused and then bowed his head. "Dear Jesus, we are so grateful for another day You have blessed us with. Thank You that Mrs. Bagwell was able to join us. We lift up church tomorrow, that You would allow us to make a difference in the nursing home. I'm reminded of Mr. McGovern and his leg that's been bothering him. Please help it to feel better. Thank You for the food we are about to eat. In Jesus' Name, Amen."

Mom handed the salad bowl to Mrs. Bagwell. "You may start this. We have several dressings to choose from." Mom showed her three bottles. "Italian, Ranch, or Honey Mustard."

Dad brought in a pan with the hamburgers, which filled the room with their delicious aroma. He handed the pan to Mom, and she took a juicy hamburger. "These look wonderful! Thank you, Sweetie."

After the hamburgers had made their round, Mitch picked up the ketchup bottle and passed it to Mrs. Bagwell. "You may start."

Mrs. Bagwell shook her head. "I'll pass."

"I think everything is better with ketchup!" Mitch encouraged.

"I know, but I'm trying to avoid acidic foods like tomatoes, because I may be allergic to them."

"That's too bad." Mitch flipped open the ketchup lid and frowned, watching the watery liquid ooze onto his plate. "It needs to be shook up."

"MITCH!" Mollie squealed, as Mitch energetically shook the bottle, and a red stream of ketchup shot toward her. Mitch stopped in mid-air but the abrupt ending only caused another spurt of ketchup to come out.

Mrs. Bagwell's glasses perched on the edge of her nose: "The lid must not have been closed, and what a mess this is! At least you didn't squirt me."

"Mitch," Mollie's voice did not sound happy, "you weren't being careful, and now I have ketchup all over me." Tears filled Mollie's eyes, and she tried not to cry.

Wanting to be helpful, Maddie reached over to Mollie and wiped at the red globs with her napkin. The ketchup smeared into larger circles. "Please don't, Maddie," Mollie begged. "I'll have to treat the jumper and have it washed. All because Mitch wasn't being careful."

Maddie seemed sad. "I was only trying to help. Maybe if I use napkin water that'll be better." She dipped her napkin into the cup and offered the soggy napkin to Mollie, but Mollie only frowned.

"I know you're sad about your jumper," Dad gently said, "but you don't need to have a bad attitude about it. Why don't you go and change, and take a minute to pray, asking the Lord to help you have loving responses?"

"Yes, sir." Mollie still looked like she was on the verge of crying, but she slipped from the table quietly.

Dad looked at several spots on the ceiling. "I'm SO sorry, Dad," Mitch groaned, feeling his face turn as red as the ketchup. "I guess I didn't close the lid before I shook it."

"Yes, Match," Mrs. Bagwell laughed. "I just told you that. It's a known fact that you didn't close the lid. Don't be embarrassed; it can happen to anyone."

"How are we going to fix the ceiling?" Max wondered.

Mitch sighed. "Will you have to replace the entire thing?"

"No, no, it's not that bad," Dad reassured him. "I think we'll use a wet rag and hope that will fix it. If the stains are still obvious, we'll face it then." Mom brought Dad the rag, and he stood on Mollie's chair, dabbing at the ceiling. "It did a pretty good job. We will see how it looks once it has dried."

The family had resumed eating when Mollie came back. A smile was on her face, and just as she was about to say something, Mitch quickly gave her a hug. "Please forgive me,

Mollie, for my carelessness, and I should have told you I was sorry right away."

"I forgive you. Please forgive me for my bad attitude; I was wrong. Maddie, please forgive me for not being kind to you too."

Chapter 15

Time with Mrs. Bagwell

After dinner, Mom carried in a plate of chocolate chip cookies. "Mollie and Maddie made our dessert this morning." Mom paused, hearing one of the twins crying on the baby monitor. She looked at the monitor sitting on the table to decide which twin it was. "It seems Melissa is awake; you all go ahead with the cookies."

Mrs. Bagwell eyed the plate. "We'll see if they taste as good as mine."

"I remember yours," Mitch remarked, "from when you had us over; I think you'll like ours better." As soon as the words slipped from his mouth, Mitch wished he could take them back. "What I was trying to say is that yours are good, but Mollie has a way of making first-class cookies."

"I'll see." A twinkle in Mrs. Bagwell's eyes told Mitch she wasn't offended.

The phone rang, and Dad answered it. "Hi . . . Well, we were about to have dessert, but that's fine . . . Okay. . ." Dad turned to the children and Mrs. Bagwell. "It's Mom's brother, Uncle Nate; we don't have the chance to talk much, so I'll take the call. I'm going upstairs; you all may finish off the cookies while I'm away."

The children chatted with Mrs. Bagwell for a while, and one by one, they found themselves reaching for a third. Mrs. Bagwell sighed. "I can't believe I'm eating three, but, Match, you're right, Mollie does make the best cookies."

"I thought you'd think so," Mitch smiled. "At least we didn't eat them all, because Mom hasn't eaten hers."

Finally, Max said, "We'd better start cleanup. Mrs. Bagwell, you may sit and watch us. I'll bring a chair into the kitchen for you."

Mrs. Bagwell raised an eyebrow. "Just sit and watch? Of course not! I'm not that old, Mix. Remember I'm from the days where people worked hard; I'll wash."

Mollie picked up the dishwashing soap from underneath the sink. "Would you like an apron?"

"No. A little soap and warm water doesn't hurt anyone." She ran the water until it reached the desired temperature, put the stopper in the bottom of the sink, and squeezed a generous amount of soap into the warm water. "Now, all I need is that stack of dishes," she instructed, adjusting her glasses with a wet hand. Max placed several items next to her. "What about all those plates?" Mrs. Bagwell pointed a finger dripping with water in the direction of the plates.

"Those go in the dishwasher," Max informed her.

"I have the dish water right here!" Mrs. Bagwell misunderstood Max.

"What I mean is we put the dishes in this dish*washer*." Max emphasized the last portion of the word, and he opened the dishwasher.

"Sorry. My hearing isn't so great, and I left my hearing aids at home! Well, let me have at those other dishes." Mrs. Bagwell moved right into another conversation, telling stories from her childhood days.

When they were done, they went into the living room. "Mrs. Bagwell," Max started, "I remember when we visited you, you told us that your husband didn't really like music.

We don't know much about your husband: would you tell us about him?"

A long pause followed. It seemed tears were filling her eyes, although Max couldn't tell for sure. "Thank you for asking," she said. Her voice became quieter. "He was a kind man and took wonderful care of me. He worked downtown managing a grocery store for many years, until it went out of business. Then he had to drive to the bigger city each day for work. My husband was a hard worker, and he was always on the lookout for odd jobs to bring in more money. One year, he surprised me and the children by taking us on a vacation! We hadn't gone for many years, and he'd been carefully saving money. When he was about fifty, he got religious. I figured if religion made him better, so be it. Only two years later, my husband was killed by a drunk driver." Mrs. Bagwell paused and shook her head. "Don't you children EVER drink— EVER! Even when you're an adult—don't! It's an awful thing. The drunk driver forever changed my life."

There was a stunned silence, as the children realized the sadness that overshadowed Mrs. Bagwell's past. Mom had heard the conversation as she stood near the stairs, holding Melissa. "I'm so sorry, Mrs. Bagwell."

Mrs. Bagwell shrugged her shoulders. "I still remember the day when I appeared in court for the man's trial. He seemed sorry but being sorry didn't help; my husband was dead. The man was sentenced to twenty-five years in prison. I couldn't make myself go back to playing music after my husband died; I felt too sad. When he died, it seemed a part of me did too."

Dad walked down the stairs with Moses, and he sensed a serious conversation. Mrs. Bagwell spoke again. "I can tell everyone is feeling sorry for me, but don't. I'm okay, really I am. I wasn't for quite a few years; the pain has lessened as time has gone on, but I've not forgotten, and I never will!

Let's go to more pleasant subjects. Jim, how'd your talk with your relative go?"

Since Dad hadn't caught the story, Dad decided Mitch would tell him all about it later. "We had a great visit. Nate was wondering how we were doing with the twins. I'm sorry I was on the phone and couldn't help with cleanup. Since that's done, would you like to join us for our family Bible time? We'd love to have you!"

"Do what now?"

"We're going to have family Bible time."

"A family what now?"

"Bible time: it's when we read the Bible together and discuss it. We'd love for you to stay."

"Oh, sorry, I don't hear well, and I left my hearing aids at the house. Oliver mentioned you do something along those lines. I didn't know what he meant by that, and I wasn't about to ask. Sure, I'll stay."

Mitch was anxious for a chance to hold Moses, so he whispered to Dad, "May I please hold him?"

"As long as you'll pay attention." Dad knew Mitch would be more inclined to play with Moses then to follow along where they were reading.

"Oh, that's right!" Mollie exclaimed. "Mom hasn't eaten her dessert! Dad, may I please get her cookies?"

"Go ahead. Normally we don't eat in here, but Mom is careful, so I'll make an exception."

Mollie warmed up Mom's cookies in the microwave, and she brought Mom the plate and a glass of milk. "I want to tell you something," Mrs. Bagwell said. "Snickers died."

Maddie's face instantly was concerned. "He died? How did he die? That's terribly sad."

"In his sleep. I've made a decision not to get another one. He took time and money for his upkeep. I do watch my money, although I'm not quite the penny-pincher like Oliver. Besides, no rat can replace Snickers."

"I know what you should buy," Maddie proposed. "You should get a duck."

All the Moodys looked incredulously at Maddie. "A duck?" Dad tried to keep a straight face.

Mrs. Bagwell nodded. "I'll have to think about it; what an interesting idea!"

Maddie tucked a curl behind her ear. "We just feeded them at the park, and I really like them. Maybe the park would give you one."

"I don't think they would," Mrs. Bagwell decided. "One of my favorite places is the farm store, and I imagine they have them there. But, I'm not sure I want a duck. I guess I'll have to chew on that idea for awhile."

Dad opened his Bible. "If you do get a duck, we'll come see it. All right, it's time for the most important part of our day. We're in James 2. Whose night is it?" Each evening, taking turns from the youngest to the oldest, it was someone's night to do four things during Bible time: open in prayer, be the first to read two verses, choose what direction around the room they would go when they each shared their application verse, and pick a hymn to sing.

"It was mine last night," Mom smiled. "That would make it yours, Dear."

"Great! I love my night. Let's open with a word of prayer. Dear Heavenly Father, another day is finishing up, and I want to thank You for our time with Mrs. Bagwell. We pray that we would focus on You tonight, and that our hearts would be listening for what You want us to learn. In Jesus' Name, Amen. James 2. 'My brethren, have not the faith of our Lord Jesus Christ, *the Lord* of glory, with respect of persons. For if there come unto your assembly a man with a gold ring, in goodly apparel, and there come in also a poor man in vile raiment.'"

"Daddy, I know Dudly. He's the mailman." Maddie was really working to pay attention to Bible time.

"I don't think his name is Dudly," Dad said to Maddie. "This is actually talking about a man in goodly apparel, which means he was wearing very fancy clothes."

"Oh."

"These next two verses are really long, so I'll read verse three, and then you may repeat verse four after me. 'And ye have respect to him that weareth the gay clothing, and say unto him, Sit thou here in a good place; and say to the poor, Stand thou there, or sit here under my footstool.' It's your turn, Maddie. 'Are ye not then partial in yourselves…"

Maddie slowly repeated: "Are ye not then partial in yourselves…"

"And are become judges of evil thoughts?"

"'And are become judges of evil thoughts?' Daddy, what does all that stuff mean?" Although Maddie couldn't read, she was still able to take part in the reading by repeating what Dad told her.

"We're going to see if Max can explain them to us."

Max pondered the verses. "I think it's saying that we treat people who have more money and look nice better than we would a poor person, who doesn't have much money and might be dressed in old clothes."

"Good. Who can think of an example?" Dad noticed Mitch smiling and tickling Moses. "Ummm, Mitch. Remember, it's Bible time."

Mitch glanced up. "I'm sorry, Dad. He's just so cute! I have an example. Last Sunday, when we were at the nursing home, there were two men sitting in the hallway. One was dressed nicely, and the other one looked like he was still in his pajamas. The well-dressed man was friendly and kind, and the other man wasn't mean, but I wouldn't call him friendly either. After we brought them in to church, Mr. Parker talked right away with the man in his pajamas, and he was aware the man was a little grouchy. I was glad Mr. Parker talked to him, because I really wanted to speak to the nicer-looking guy. I was showing partiality."

"That's exactly right," Dad agreed.

Mitch shot a look at Mrs. Bagwell, wondering what she thought of their Bible time; her face seemed serious, but he couldn't tell any other emotion. After Mitch read, Mrs. Bagwell said, "I'll listen," and patted Mollie. Mollie read the next two verses, and it was Max's turn on nine and ten.

"But if ye have respect to persons, ye commit sin, and are convinced of the law as transgressors. For whosoever shall keep the whole law, and yet offend in one *point*, he is guilty of all."

"Dad," Mitch began, "didn't Grandpa use this verse when he talked to Mr. Delome about his salvation?"

"He might have; I don't know since I wasn't there. This verse is saying if we break one of God's commandments—even just one—we are a law breaker, and we're guilty."

When it was Mollie's turn again, she was on verses nineteen and twenty. "Thou believest that there is one God; thou doest well: the devils also believe, and tremble. But wilt thou know, O vain man, that faith without works is dead?"

"Verse nineteen is what the Lord used to really shake me up," Dad told the family. "I believed in God, yet when my friend was witnessing to me, he shared this verse, and it said the devils also believe. I knew then there was a problem. The devils aren't saved, and if they believe in God, what was the difference in our beliefs? It wasn't enough to believe in God. I had to realize I was a sinner, deserving of hell and personally believe that Jesus died on the cross for my sins." Soon, the chapter was finished, and Dad said, "We'll stop there tonight. I chose verse four: 'Are ye not then partial in yourselves, and are become judges of evil thoughts?' With my work at the bank, this can easily happen. An unkempt person comes in, and I know at first glance they likely will only take my time and not do any business with us. I can feel begrudging of their questions when I have other things to do. But, the Lord doesn't call me to choose whom I'd rather help: the nice-looking person or the scraggly guy. I'll go . . . let's see . . . Mom's way."

"Thanks. I chose verse seventeen. I want to truly serve others and show my love for the Lord Jesus through my actions, not just my words."

Max sighed. "I'm having a hard time deciding between two. I guess I'll do verse fourteen, about faith and works. I want to show others that I am trusting in Jesus for my salvation, and it's not only something I'm saying, but Jesus is real in my life."

Mrs. Bagwell motioned Mollie to go. "I like number eight," Mollie said. "You and Mom encourage us to love each other and be kind, and that is what I want."

Mitch laid Moses on the floor next to him. "He's trying to go to sleep. Should I keep him awake?"

"Yes, please."

Mitch picked him back up. "You need to stay awake, little guy." Mitch made a funny face, but Moses only yawned.

"Mitch," Dad reminded.

Mitch quickly responded, "Sorry, I forgot it was my turn. Dad, I like yours. I don't want to be critical of others or desire to be only around nice people."

Dad patted Maddie. "Do you have a verse?"

"I like eight, same as Mollie's, but I chose it before she did, because I want to love my neighbors. Mommy says that my brothers and sisters are my neighbors too, so I need to love them." Even though Maddie couldn't read, she watched each

"An unkempt person comes in, and I know at first glance they likely will only take my time and not do any business with us."

person as they read, and she kept track of the verse numbers. When they read a verse she liked, she remembered the number.

"Does anyone have an offense they need to deal with—something that you should ask forgiveness for?" Dad closed his Bible.

"I do," Maddie said. She looked slightly shy, glancing at Mrs. Bagwell. "Mollie, I used your brush and forgot to put it away. When you were looking for it, I didn't tell you I knew where it was. It's in the closet. Please forgive me."

"I forgive you."

"Max, would you pass out the hymn books? I've decided we're going to begin using them, and that way we can sing all the verses of the hymn, and hopefully learn more that way."

"Yes, sir." Max promptly found the stack of red hymnals.

Dad flipped through the pages. "'Let the Lower Lights be Burning,' page 371."

When they were done singing, Mrs. Bagwell stood up. "I really hate to be leaving, because I enjoyed myself very much. It's remarkable the children understand the depth of the reading."

"We were glad you could come," Dad encouraged.

"Me too. It's much better than eating by one's self. At any rate, my stomach has been bothering me lately, and I need to take my Pepto-Bismol before I go to bed."

"We're sorry to hear that. I hope dinner didn't aggravate it." Mom sounded concerned.

"Don't you worry—it does this every evening. Good-bye!"

Chapter 16

The Animal Catcher

One quiet summer morning, Max was watching Maddie and the twins. "You may hold Melissa if you sit on the couch," Max instructed.

Maddie bounced around in excitement. "I like to hold babies."

After giving Melissa to Maddie, Max sat on the floor next to Moses, who had learned to roll over only a day after Melissa. He enjoyed doing it so much he no longer stayed on the blanket. Max found a toy to coax Moses closer to him.

"Max, what's that big cat doing there?" Maddie could see out the front window from her viewpoint on the couch.

"It's probably just a stray."

"It's a very fat cat with stripes on its tail."

Max picked Moses up and looked where Maddie pointed. "Oh, wow! That's a raccoon!"

"A ratoon? May I go see it?"

"No." Max didn't catch Maddie's misunderstanding of the word. He wondered why the raccoon would be outside in the middle of the day. The raccoon waddled in circles around a small area. "Something is wrong with it. I would call Mom, but I might scare the twins." Max laid Moses on the floor and then took Melissa from Maddie. "Please get Mom; she's in her room, and I'll stay here."

"Okay!" Maddie nodded, skipping off.

Mollie and Mitch were in the kitchen working on lunch, when Maddie called to them, "Hurry to the living room! There's a ratoon!"

Mitch almost fell running into the living room to see the action. "Maddie's saying something about a rat! The only rat I know is Snickers, and he's dead!" Before Max could respond, Mitch said, "That's not a rat—that's a raccoon!"

Mom joined the group at the window to observe the raccoon. "What do you think, Mom?" Max asked.

"The raccoon seems to have a big problem. Dad called a few minutes ago, and he's on his way home for lunch. He'll have to decide what to do, but I'm sure he'll call Animal Control."

"Oh, good!" Mitch exclaimed. "I hope they send Mr. Gibson! We haven't seen him for a while."

The raccoon continued to walk in circles, and it would often lose its balance and fall over. Dad pulled into the driveway and saw the family gathered around the window. It didn't take him long to see where they were looking. He parked in the garage, and Mitch met him at the door. "Guess what, Dad? There's a raccoon in our yard!"

"I saw that," Dad said. He followed Mitch into the house, stopping to pat Maple, who was excited he was home. "Raccoons aren't usually out during the day."

"Right. It's because they're nocturnal animals," Mitch explained. "They sleep during the day and are awake at night. This one must be sick."

Max stepped back from the window so there would be room for Dad to look out. "I need to call Animal Control," was Dad's only remark.

"I'll find the number." Mitch ran for the phone directory.

After Dad called, he reported on his conversation. "They transferred me to Mr. Gibson's cell phone, and he said he'll be by in a few minutes. He was on his way to lunch, but he'll stop here first."

"Would you please help me carry the twins upstairs, Jim? I need to feed them," Mom said. "I'm sure I won't be needed for the raccoon adventure," she laughed.

"May we go out and watch the raccoon?" begged Mitch.

Dad shook his head. "Just wait. I'll help Mom, and we'll go together when Mr. Gibson arrives." A few minutes later, Mr. Gibson parked his animal catcher truck on the driveway.

"So what do ya have here?" Mr. Gibson drawled as he saw the children trailing behind Dad.

"A raccoon showed up in our yard sometime this morning," Dad explained.

The large raccoon staggered to its feet and continued his circle walking. "He is sick," Mr. Gibson pronounced, sticking his hands into his overall pockets. "You were smart to call me." He lumbered to the back of his truck, rummaging around before he found a cage. Then, he opened a side door and pulled out a long metal pole with an adjustable

The large raccoon staggered to its feet
and continued his circle walking.

noose at the end. "I brought my handy-dandy catch pole. If this was jist a normal situation, and you had a coon that was bein' a nuisance, we'd bait us a trap. Since this fellar is a sick one, we have to use this to catch him. It'd be mighty foolish to let him stay loose."

Mr. Gibson stepped into the grass, and as he approached the raccoon, he laid the wire cage on the ground and unlatched the door. Then he thrust the long metal pole toward the raccoon and slipped the noose over its neck. Mr. Gibson gently directed the sick creature into the cage and carefully disengaged the noose. He hurried to latch the door. "All taken care of. You do have interestin' creatures for me—if I rightly remember, it was a deer last fall. Least ways it gives me an excuse to see you. I still remember that dinner I had at yore house when yer ma was expectin'. Where's them twins?" Mr. Gibson lifted the cage into one of the side compartments of his truck and shut the door with a firm clank.

"They're inside," Dad replied. "We would love to have you join us for lunch, if you're able."

Mr. Gibson pulled a tarnished silver watch from his overall pocket. "I reckon I would if I could, but I'm plum out of time. My boss told me to make sure I was back before one o'clock for a meetin' otherwise I know I'd git hollered at. It's 'bout more city rules, but they have a nicer word for it."

"Could we at least send you with lunch?"

"Dependin' on what it is," Mr. Gibson teased with a twinkle in his eyes.

"It's yummy," Maddie spoke for the first time. "Tuna fishy sandwiches!"

Mr. Gibson's grin grew bigger. "That'd be right tolerable."

Mollie hurried in the house to pack his lunch. Mr. Gibson crossed his arms and leaned against the truck. "Work's keepin' me right busy 'cause it's only me and one other fellar. I've still been considerin' retirin'," Mr. Gibson paused. "Someday I'll live the good life."

"This is a little off topic, but where do you go to church?" Dad asked.

"I don't. I have mowin' to do on Saturdays, and then I take it real easy on Sundays. I know it's in the good book to have a day of rest."

"Do you ever think about spiritual things?"

Mr. Gibson grabbed his handkerchief from his pocket to mop his forehead. "Lately, I have been. My older brother tries to talk to me 'bout those sorts of things; I guess you know him—my niece, Carolyn, is your baby nurse, or whatever ya call them." Mr. Gibson cleared his throat. "I guess I'll tell you. I'm not a prayin' type of fellar, but I know you folks are. You could pray for my wife. Early on this month, the doctors told us she has a bad kind of cancer, and the doctors don't expect her to make it through the end of the year." He shook his head. "I jist don't get it." Mr. Gibson used his handkerchief to wipe his eyes.

Dad put a hand on Mr. Gibson's shoulder. "We're very sorry to hear this. We will be praying. Please let us know if you need anything."

"Thanks."

Just then, Mollie came out and handed Mr. Gibson a small brown bag. "Here's your lunch," she cheerfully said, unaware of the serious conversation.

"I'm much obliged."

Mr. Gibson climbed in his truck, backed from the driveway, and disappeared down the street. "I can hardly believe it!"

Max exclaimed. "I've never met his wife, but what if she's not saved?"

"What happened?" Mollie asked Mitch.

"We'll tell you when we tell Mom!"

The family solemnly headed in and shared Mr. Gibson's news. "How sad," Mom said and snuggled Moses closer. "I'm glad he opened up so we can be praying for them. Maybe we can have them over for dinner sometime."

"Dad, I've been thinking," Mitch paused and plopped onto the floor, "about what Mr. Gibson said about the 'good life.' What does he mean by that?"

"Well, probably to Mr. Gibson the good life is that he won't have to work and can just enjoy doing whatever he wants to do. Many people live for that time in their lives."

"Oh." Mitch looked at Dad. "Are you looking forward to retirement too?"

Dad smiled. "You know, Mitch, I want to be always busy about what the Lord has for me. When the time comes to stop working an official job, that just means I'll have more time to be about the Lord's work. There'll be no retirement for your daddy."

A grin spread across Mitch's face. "I like that!"

Chapter
17

Moving Day

August 13th arrived, a day the children had been looking forward to: Grandpa and Grandma's moving day! Around six that morning, Dad walked into the boys' room. "Time to wake up," he said. "Remember, it's moving day."

Rustling was heard from Mitch's bed. "When are we leaving for Grandpa's?"

"We'll aim to get there around eight. You all may get dressed and then come downstairs for your Bible time. Mom is feeding Moses, and then he'll sleep a little longer."

Dad left the room to go to the girls'. "This *is* the day *which* Lord hath made; we will rejoice and be glad in it."

Maddie moved slightly, rubbing her eyes. "I'm still tired."

"Do you want to help Grandpa and Grandma move?"

Instantly, Maddie sat up. "Oh, yes. Is Melissa sleeping?"

"No, Mom's feeding her, but she'll put the twins back to sleep soon."

Not hearing anything from Mollie, Dad stepped over to her bed. "Mollie, are you awake?"

Mollie sighed, but it sounded more like a groan. As soon as she started talking, it was obvious she was sick. "I feel awful; my throat is on fire, and my head feels like it's stuffed with cotton."

"I'm sorry, Mollie."

Tears slid down Mollie's cheeks. "I wanted to help today," she whispered.

Dad knelt near Mollie's bed. "I know. We've all been looking forward to this move. With your head hurting, it would be best to have a quiet day at home. Why don't you try to go back to sleep for a while?"

"Yes, sir." Mollie snuggled under her covers. "Would you please find my winter blanket in the closet? I'm cold!"

"Sure." Dad walked to the closet and felt around for the blanket. He came back, draped the blanket over her, and said, "I think you may have a fever, so I'll get a thermometer." Dad came back with the thermometer.

"Thanks, Dad."

Mom was just coming out of her room. "Perfect! Would you tuck Moses in?" She handed the sleepy baby to Dad.

"Yes. By the way, Mollie is sick with a sore throat, and her head doesn't feel good."

"She is going to be so disappointed," Mom remarked. "All the children have been excited! Now that I think about it, Mollie did seem unusually tired last night, plus she had a small headache. I guess that'll change her day!"

After laying Moses in his crib, Dad went downstairs to find Maddie and the boys in the living room. Maddie sat on the couch with her earphones in, intently listening to the Bible on CD. Dad chuckled to himself. Mom's idea for Maddie being able to have Bible time since she couldn't read had really worked!

When Mom came downstairs to prepare breakfast, Maddie was ready to be her helper. "I like to help you make breakfast," Maddie said.

"And I love having a helper." Mom pulled a bag of muffins from the freezer.

"Will you be all right by yourself today?" Maddie seemed truly concerned.

"Yes, I'll be fine."

Around seven, the family gathered to eat. After Dad blessed the food, Mom passed the muffins around the table. Mollie surprised them—since they thought she was sleeping—by plopping herself on the floor next to Maple. Shivering, she patted the dog. "I'm awake," she announced.

Dad spread butter on his muffin. "Did you get back to sleep?"

"Only for a little while. I took my temperature before I came down, and it's 101. Do you know what sounds good?" Mollie rubbed Maple's ears.

"Ice cream?" Mom responded.

"No, hot tea. My throat feels dreadful."

"I'll get you some." Mitch jumped up from the table, almost knocking over his drink. "What kind would you like?"

"I don't care."

"You must be very sick to want hot tea in the summer," Mitch remarked, rummaging through Mom's stash of tea bags.

"What are your plans for the day, Emily?" Dad asked.

"I think with not having help with the twins, plus being a nurse to Mollie, my day will be quite full. I'm also going to make dinner for everyone tonight, and I'll try to do a bit of laundry in between things."

"Maddie could always stay home," Max offered.

Maddie cast a glance at Max. "I want to help Grandpa and Grandma move."

"I'll be fine, Max; thanks for the concern," Mom said.

After breakfast was finished, everyone scattered to prepare to leave. Several minutes later, the moving crew was ready. "We'll take the van, I think," Dad decided as he grabbed the keys. "Love you, Emily"—he gave Mom a kiss.

As Dad backed from the garage, Mitch asked, "Is Mr. Delome helping today?"

"No. He left early this morning on a little trip to visit a friend he used to work with who lives three hours away. Mr. Delome has been praying for his salvation. The friend invited him to come for a few days. Mr. Delome really wanted to help Grandpa move, but Grandpa assured him we'd get along without him. Mr. Parker will also be helping."

"I think it's neat Mr. Delome wanted to witness to his friend," Max observed. "I forgot to tell you this, but when we were washing the van, Mr. Delome told us he witnessed to his son, and he's also been talking to Mrs. Bagwell about spiritual things!"

A little later, Dad pulled into Grandpa and Grandma's driveway and turned off the engine. "Mr. Parker's here," Mitch exclaimed.

"It's great to see you all!" Mr. Parker greeted them as he pulled a tan ball cap from his truck.

A loud rumbling was heard, and a gray moving truck with bold letters scripted across the side, spelling *U-Move,* drove slowly up. Grandpa was driving, and he honked at the group before parking on the circle drive near the front door. He hopped from the truck. "Good morning!"

"Hi, Grandpa!" several voices chorused.

"Grandpa," Mitch said, "did you know Mollie's really sick?"

"I'm sorry to hear that. Come inside; it's going to be a warm one!"

Boxes were stacked in the front area, and Grandma hurried through. "Hi! Sorry about the mess."

Grandpa laughed. "Martha, there's no mess to apologize for. What is Mollie sick with?"

"It's probably a flu bug, the kind where you get a fever and cold symptoms," Dad explained.

"I'm sorry for her." Grandpa looked around. "Well, if you all are ready, let's start with loading out furniture into the truck, and then we can put boxes in at the end."

Maddie watched as the guys set to work. "What can I do, Grandma?"

"You may help me with a few things in the kitchen."

"The couch is heavy," Grandpa cautioned to Dad and Mr. Parker.

. . . a gray moving truck with bold letters scripted across the side, spelling U-Move, drove slowly up.

Mr. Parker evaluated it. "We'll be fine. That is, if Jim can carry his side."

"Of course I can," Dad smiled.

Max went for Grandma's recliner chair. "Come on, Mitch." The boys strained as they picked up the chair.

"Careful not to drop it," Grandpa instructed, slightly concerned over the well-being of the chair.

"Yes, sir." Mitch puffed as he lifted his end higher. The boys made it through the front door and into the truck. Dad and Mr. Parker scooted out of the way as the boys carried the chair by.

They set the chair down, and Max wiped his forehead. "That was a little heavier than I thought, but we did it."

It took about an hour and a half before the first load was ready. As Max brought a box of Grandma's china dishes to the van, he remembered how his finger had been closed in Grandma's trunk the last time they moved. *I hope there are no accidents today,* he thought to himself. Grandpa, Max, and Mitch jumped into the moving truck, and Dad, Grandma, Maddie, and Mr. Parker followed in the van.

As they pulled in front of the new house, Mitch spotted Mollie in her bedroom window. "Grandpa, Mollie's waving! Please wave to her; I don't know if she can see me!"

Mollie's face brightened, returning Grandpa's wave. "Your mom and Moses are looking from the living room," Grandpa chuckled before cautiously backing into the driveway.

After they climbed out, Mitch bent down. "The truck is leaking oil; it's going to make a dark spot on your nice cement."

Grandpa sighed. "The U-Move trucks aren't in top-notch condition. I guess we'll try to find a little bucket or container to put underneath it to catch the drips."

Soon, everyone was busy carrying items into the house, and Grandpa directed where they were to go. "Grandpa," said Maddie, who had been watching him for an opportunity to talk, "I want to help carry stuff too. I'm big enough."

Grandpa thought for a moment, trying to decide if there was anything small she could carry. "We only have a few boxes in this load, but they're too heavy. Maybe next load."

Maddie nodded, following Max and Mitch out to the truck. They each picked up a dining room chair. "Are those really heavy, Max?" Maddie pushed a sweaty curl from her forehead.

"They would be for you," Max said.

When the boys were gone, Maddie strolled up the ramp into the truck and found a box sitting along the side wall. She tried to lift the box, but it *was* heavy. Straining, she tried again. This time, she succeeded, and she turned around. Not noticing a moving blanket on the floor, she tripped. The box flew from her arms, sliding to the ramp. "OHHHH!" she cried, sitting up quickly. A sting of pain caused her to lift her jumper and examine her knee. "It's bleeding!"

Dad whistled, as he walked from the garage to the ramp, but he was surprised to see a box on its side at the top. "I wonder why—oh, Maddie, what happened?" He moved the box and knelt next to her.

"I hurt my knee. See, it's bleeding."

"Let's go over to our house where Mom can clean it for you." Dad picked Maddie up, and Maddie began sobbing. "Does it hurt that bad?" Dad wondered.

"No, but I disobeyed Grandpa."

"Is that what happened? It's important to obey. Now you see consequences for not obeying Grandpa. After Mom takes care of your knee, you need to ask Grandpa's forgiveness for disobeying."

"Yes, sir," Maddie sniffled while wiping her tears.

Dad stepped into the house where Mom was in the living room folding clothes. "What's the matter?" Mom set the laundry basket to the side.

"Maddie fell." Dad carried Maddie to the kitchen. "Do you want her on the floor?"

"Sure."

"How is Mollie?"

"She may be doing a little better. She slept for a while, and I found a biography for her to read, so she likes that. Her fever was about 100 last I checked. I set up the portable crib for Melissa to sleep in our room; being out of the room might help her not get sick, plus Mollie won't have to keep the light off and be quiet during Melissa's nap times."

"Good plan; I'd better be going. Love you." With that, Dad left.

Mom took a clean washcloth, ran it under cool water, and gently wiped Maddie's knee. "Ouch," Maddie tensed. "It really hurts, Mommy. Do you know what I did?"

"Dad said you fell."

"Yes. Grandpa told me I couldn't carry a box, but I wanted to, and then I felled."

Mom spread a thin layer of antibiotic ointment on Maddie's knee. "Sometimes you experience natural consequences for disobedience." Mom placed two band aids over the affected area. "You're all fixed up."

"Thanks, Mommy; I'm ready to go back."

"Be a good girl," Mom instructed. "This time, obey what others tell you!"

"Yes, ma'am!" Maddie agreed.

Mom watched her little girl skip to Grandpa and Grandma's house. "Bye, Mommy!" Maddie called. She walked into Grandpa and Grandma's garage and found Grandpa. "Please forgive me, Grandpa. I didn't obey you 'cause I carried a box."

"I forgive you. Now, run along to the kitchen to help your grandma."

Chapter
18

A Delay

By midafternoon, there was only one truckload left to fetch from Grandpa's old house to complete the move. "It looks like your dad and the others have a head start on us," Grandpa observed as he and Mitch clambered up into the truck for the final trip. "I didn't realize we were so behind!"

Soon, Mitch remarked: "I'm hungry; lunch didn't go far enough in my stomach."

"You should have asked Grandma for a snack if you were hungry," Grandpa almost scolded. "If we were in my truck, you could have opened the glove box and found yourself a package of peanut butter crackers."

"I'll be okay. Mom is making tacos for dinner, and I'll fill up then!" Mitch paused and changed the topic: "I've been praying for Mrs. Gibson this afternoon while we worked."

"We were sad to hear about her cancer," Grandpa remarked. "I was thinking back to when I shared the gospel with Oliver. I used the example that he was headed toward a fire much worse than a house fire—and it was my job to warn him. I wonder what the Gibsons' spiritual state is."

Mitch shook his head. "Mr. Gibson doesn't seem very interested in things of the Lord. Grandpa, just think. If Mrs. Gibson isn't saved, she's headed for hell! That's awful! I'm going to pray even more for her salvation!" Several minutes later, Mitch wondered if he saw a puff of smoke rise from the engine. "Grandpa, I think our engine is smoking!"

"I don't see anything," Grandpa cast a sweeping glance over the hood.

"I thought I saw smoke, but maybe it was only heat radiating from the cement." Mitch opened his window farther to get a better air current moving through the hot truck.

"Hopefully the truck will stay together long enough for us to finish," Grandpa dryly remarked. "I wish there had been another place to rent from than U-Move; they've not impressed me with their trucks, but Sunflower only had one choice."

Suddenly, white smoke began pouring out of the hood. "Oh, no!" Grandpa hollered. "We do have a problem!" They were coming up to a side street, and Grandpa quickly turned onto it.

Mitch's eyes widened as the smoke rose in billows. Grandpa shut off the truck, and his voice sounded tense. "I want you to get out and away from the truck!"

Mitch obediently threw open his door and hopped down. In his excitement, he tumbled to the grass. "I know where the fire extinguisher is!" Mitch called.

Grandpa grabbed his furniture-moving gloves from the truck and hurried to the engine. "Not yet. Just stay back. I'm checking to see if we're dealing with a fire or a mechanical issue." He fumbled to feel for the hood release, and the hood popped open.

Mitch prayed silently as he watched from a safe distance. At first, smoke billowed from the engine, but it quickly lessened. "It's not a fire," Grandpa sighed in relief. "You may come over."

"It's hot!" Mitch exclaimed, as he felt the heat rise from the engine.

Grandpa pulled his cell phone from his pocket. "I should have U-Move's number from when I called them yesterday." He scrolled through his recent calls and found it. Several minutes later, Grandpa had called U-Move and Dad. "After all that, U-Move doesn't have another truck available. They said to put the key in the glove box, and they'll come by. You know, Mitch, let's pray together. I'm feeling stressed about all this, not to mention I'm cooking in this heat." They stepped to a shady area next to the road and bowed their heads.

It took a little while before the familiar sight of the Moodys' van was seen. Dad, Max, and Mr. Parker jumped out. "It's a good thing we didn't have the truck loaded," Mr. Parker commented as they walked to where Grandpa and Mitch stood.

"I'm glad too," Grandpa agreed. "Are Grandma and Maddie at our old house?"

Dad nodded. "They had a few things to do."

"We might as well call it quits for the day. We'll finish up on a weekday evening or next Saturday, because I'm not going to do it on Sunday."

At first, smoke billowed from the engine . . .

As they climbed in the van, a pickup truck drove by. Mitch saw brake lights come on as the driver noticed the truck hood open. Throwing his truck in reverse, the man rolled down his window to talk to Dad. "Are you guys havin' problems?" The man who called to them looked to be in his early twenties, clean-shaven and with brown hair.

"My parents are moving, and the truck we rented broke down."

There was a pause. "You look familiar," the young man noted. "Have you been to the zoo before?"

"Yes, in January." It suddenly dawned on Dad who he was talking to: George, a zookeeper, whom they had met on Mom and Maddie's birthday. "I remember you now, George, but I didn't recognize you without a beard or zookeeper clothes!" Dad chuckled.

"I know; I shaved it off earlier this summer. I'm not normally in Sunflower, but I was helping a friend train his dog today. Do you have any more loads?" George asked.

"Only one, but we'll take care of it next week."

"I don't have any time pressures tonight, and I'd be happy to take a load or two wherever you need it," George offered.

Dad glanced at Grandpa. "With my truck," Grandpa said, "and Jason's, and now George's, we could finish out the move." Grandpa leaned forward to make eye contact with George. "I don't want to impose on you, but if you're willing, we'd be grateful."

"Absolutely. I heard they're calling for bad storms tonight, so the sooner the better. Where are we headed?"

"Back to the old house: we'll lead the way," Grandpa responded.

George followed them, and a little later, they pulled into the circle drive. He grinned at the children as he climbed out.

"You all need to come to the zoo again; we have a new baby gorilla, and boy is he cool!"

After the three trucks were loaded, several long straps were fastened on each truck bed to keep things from moving around. Mitch observed the darkening sky. "George was right," he said quietly to Max. "I think I see a thunderhead over there." Mitch continued to keep tabs on the weather as they drove to Grandpa's new house. "If it does rain, your things will get soaked," Mitch decided as he rode in Grandpa's truck.

"Why don't you pray the Lord holds off the rain?" Grandpa requested. "At least until we can get things inside." Mitch prayed aloud as Grandpa drove.

When they arrived at the new house, Grandpa parked in the street so George and Mr. Parker's pickup trucks could be unloaded first. Dad pulled the van into the Moodys' driveway. Several drops of rain hit the cement as Grandpa jumped from his truck. "We need to hurry. Let's get one side of the garage cleared so we can unload everything in there!" It only took a few minutes before the garage was ready, and then Mr. Parker backed his truck a little closer to help with unloading. As they raced to unload the items, Mitch wasn't sure they were going to make it. *Please Lord,* Mitch prayed silently, *help the rain to hold off.*

When Mr. Parker's truck was empty, they worked on George's. Rumbles of thunder sounded like they were coming close, and lightning flashed across the sky, but it continued only to sprinkle. Grandpa tossed the keys to Dad and told him, "You can get my truck."

Sweat poured down their faces while they worked on unloading Grandpa's truck. Finally, the last item was a tool chest on wheels. Dad pushed it toward the tailgate where Grandpa, Mr. Parker, and George lifted it out. Just as they set it down, a wall of rain swept over the driveway. Wind whipped around the yard, sending a cool breeze into the garage. Mr. Parker quickly pushed the chest into the garage as several flashes of lightning were followed by a crash of thunder. Grandpa wiped his forehead, "Praise the Lord! We made it!"

Grandma invited them inside for something cold to drink. "We have soda or bottled water," she said, looking in the refrigerator.

George chatted with them while he drank his soda. Maddie had been watching him quietly. "Do you know Jesus?" she boldly asked him, surprising everyone with her question.

George shrugged his shoulders. "I know a little about Him. Do you?"

Maddie smiled. "Daddy tells me about Him. I'm not saved yet, but I've been listening to Daddy preach."

"Oh. Are you a pastor?" George asked Dad.

"I guess you could say that. We have Sunday morning services at a nursing home."

George furrowed his eyebrows. "Hmmmm. That is interesting. You know, I'm wondering if you were the one to talk to me about religious things at the zoo."

Dad nodded. "I thought so," George said. "I talk to so many people I didn't remember that at first. You also encouraged me to read the Bible. I haven't, but maybe I will."

"We'd love to have you visit church sometime," Mr. Parker encouraged.

George shrugged his shoulders. "I might. Why don't you give me your e-mail address, and if I'm interested, I'll drop you a note."

Chapter
19
Two Phone Calls

Several days later, the Moodys gathered around the table. After Dad blessed the food, Mitch remarked, "It's too bad Maddie and Melissa are sick now too; I hope I don't get it!"

"Being sick is miserable," Mollie dumped a spoonful of broccoli casserole on her plate. "I feel better even though my nose is still stuffy."

Dad took a serving of casserole. "I take it Maddie is sleeping."

"Yes, she is. She doesn't have much of an appetite, but I'll see if she'll eat something after we're through." Mom looked down at Melissa in the sling. "Her little nose is running," Mom wiped it with a napkin. "I think she has a slight fever as well. Oh! I've been meaning to mention this, but I'm loving the girls' sunflowers! I can see them from my bedroom window, and they are just beautiful."

Mollie nodded. "I've enjoyed watching them grow, too!"

The phone rang, and Dad stepped into the kitchen to answer it. He was soon back. "That was Mrs. Bagwell, and she's in the hospital!"

"Oh, no!" Mollie cried. "Why is she there?"

"Mrs. Bagwell said she's not been feeling well for a few months, although the last two weeks have been much worse. She asked if we could come see her. I assured her we would: I think I'll take Max. I wish Mom could go, but with Maddie and Melissa sick, we don't want Grandma watching them and possibly catching it."

Mom nodded. "You're right."

The phone rang again. "Now who could that be?" Dad wondered. After his conversation, Dad reported, "Grandma wanted to know how the sick ones were feeling. She said she received a busy signal when she tried calling a little while ago; I told her about Mrs. Bagwell's call. She immediately offered to watch the children. Actually, she all but insisted she wanted to come over, so that Mom can go to the hospital with me. She said not to worry about her getting sick. Max, we'll leave you home since Mom is going with me, and Grandma will be here. Emily," Dad continued. "If you're through with dinner, why don't you go feed the twins a little early so we can have Bible time right after that? I'm afraid if we delay it, we'll have a late evening."

"Sure." Mom hurried from the table.

In the meantime, conversation revolved around Mrs. Bagwell. "Do you think she's at the same hospital as Grandma was with her heart attack?" Mitch wondered.

"Yes," Dad said. Soon the family started on cleanup, and after Mom was done with the twins, Dad helped her bring them down to the living room. When the Moodys had finished their special time in God's Word, Dad called Grandma, while the children finished cleanup. "Let's sing a song," suggested Mollie. "Although I won't be able to sing much, because my cold makes it hard."

Mitch found a container to put the leftover casserole in. "How about 'When the Roll Is Called Up Yonder'?"

"I'll start." Max hummed and then began, "When the trumpet of the Lord shall sound. . ."

Soon, Grandma came over. "Thank you so much for taking care of the children," Mom gave Moses to Grandma. "I usually feed the twins at nine and then put them to bed. We will be home before that; Melissa is sleeping in the small crib in my room. I'm watching her closely since she's sick: here's the baby monitor. She's been pretty fussy, but I think she'll be okay for you. I just checked on Maddie and gave her some juice and crackers."

"Sounds good, Emily. Don't worry—we'll be fine."

It was a warm summer evening, and the sun was slowly setting as Dad backed the car from the garage. Mom commented, "It feels strange to leave without the children. The last time was right before the twins were born."

Several minutes later, they arrived at the hospital. Dad and Mom's shoes squeaked as they walked across the shiny floor. "Stairs or elevator?" Dad asked Mom.

"I would like the exercise of going up the stairs."

It didn't take long before they stepped onto the second floor. Going a short way down the brightly lit hall, they found Room 210. A nurse happened to be coming from the room with a tray of mostly untouched food. "Hello," she greeted them kindly. "May I help you?"

"We've come to see Maud Bagwell."

"Go on in; she finished what little dinner she would eat."

Mrs. Bagwell weakly smiled. Her normally curly hair was straight, and her skin had a grayish tint to it. Mom gently took Mrs. Bagwell's hand in hers. "We were sad to hear you're not feeling well."

"Thank you." Mrs. Bagwell closed her eyes. "I've been taking Pepto-Bismol for a few months now. The last two weeks have been horrible, and I was even running a fever off and on. I felt so awful I went to the doctor. He sent me straight over here to be admitted."

Mom noticed Mrs. Bagwell seemed to have lost weight. Mrs. Bagwell continued: "The doctor said he's going to do surgery tomorrow morning. He thinks it might be my gallbladder, but the only way for him to be able to tell will be to do surgery."

"I'm sure you'll be all right. Gallbladder surgery is pretty common and not very serious," Dad said.

Mrs. Bagwell nodded. "My car is in the doctor's office section of this parking lot, and I don't want it left there. Would you or Emily drive it home? There's no need for it to sit here while I have surgery and then recover. I parked in the second row toward the middle." She reached for her purse, which was sitting on a tray. Digging around, she pulled out a set of keys. "That section of the lot isn't too big, and you know the vehicle."

"Of course we will," Dad assured her. "I can't believe you drove yourself here. Please, if you have a need like this again, call us, and we'll be happy to take you."

"I appreciate that, but I like to do things for myself, besides the fact that I dislike inconveniencing people." After a few minutes of chit chat, Mrs. Bagwell sighed and pulled at the white sheet. "I haven't told you everything. It's probably more than a simple surgery to fix my gallbladder. The doctor says he's 95 percent sure I have cancer, and there's nothing that can be done. Everything points to cancer. The only way to tell if it is, is to go in and do the surgery, and see what condition I'm in." Mrs. Bagwell paused. "He also said if it is cancer, there are no good treatment options for how advanced it would be, and I wouldn't have long to live."

"Mrs. Bagwell, I'm sorry!" Mom exclaimed, gently squeezing Mrs. Bagwell's hand.

"Don't be. I'm an old lady, and maybe it's my time to—" she paused and swallowed hard. "Die. There, I said it. Ever since my husband died, I don't like to say that word. Oliver has been talking to me about Jesus, the Bible, 'getting saved,' and so on. I tried to act like I understood, but the reality is, I don't. I've always hoped I will go to heaven. I've believed God will understand that we're all human and not perfect. I don't think I've done anything to deserve hell; I mean, sure, I'm a little crusty, but nothing awful. The drunk driver, now he's a different story. What Oliver has been telling me has made me start to question if what I've believed is accurate."

Dad's heart jumped as he realized he now had a perfect opportunity to share with Mrs. Bagwell. He pulled his Soul Winner's New Testament from his pocket and flipped through it. "Would you be able to read Bible verses aloud, if I open to the right page?" Dad asked Mrs. Bagwell.

"With my glasses I could. They are on the tray." Mrs. Bagwell seemed interested, and she used the control to raise her bed up.

He pulled his Soul Winner's New Testament from his pocket and flipped through it.

Mom handed the glasses to Mrs. Bagwell. Dad held out the New Testament, and Mrs. Bagwell took it. She read 2 Corinthians 5:21: "For he hath made him *to be* sin for us, who knew no sin; that we might be made the righteousness of God in him." Mrs. Bagwell raised an eyebrow. "What does that mean?"

"That means that God made Jesus to take our sin on Him— He had never sinned, thus the part 'who knew no sin.' Jesus became the sacrifice for our sins—but it's only for those who will receive Him. Here's Romans 3:23, a short but important verse."

Mrs. Bagwell adjusted her glasses and slowly read, "For all have sinned, and come short of the glory of God." She paused. "Everyone sins. Isn't He a forgiving God? I haven't done anything awful, like what a person goes to jail for."

"Are you familiar with the Ten Commandments?"

"Sort of—my grandparents taught them to me when I was growing up."

"The Ten Commandments are God's law, and He will judge us based on them. One of the commandments is 'Thou shalt not covet.' Have you ever wanted something that is not yours?"

"Of course. Haven't we all?"

"Yes. Another one is 'Thou shalt not steal.' That means anything that's not your own, even a paperclip. We could go through each commandment, and you and I would be guilty of all ten. Even the commandment that says, 'Thou shalt not kill.'"

Before Dad could go on, Mrs. Bagwell shook her head. "You're wrong; of course you nor I have done that."

"Correct, but in the New Testament, Jesus said if I am angry with someone, I have committed murder in my heart. We have all broken God's law. That's the very bad news, but there is also very good news. Jesus Christ paid your fine on the cross many years ago, and that means that God, the Judge, can legally dismiss your case. The fine is only paid, though, if you will accept His offer of the free gift of salvation."

"I had never thought of it like that. I always thought God would forgive me because I am human, and we all sin. This is making sense—please keep going."

Just then, a knock was heard, and a nurse walked in. "I hope I'm not interrupting anything," she said. Her voice sounded cheerful. "I need to check Mrs. Bagwell's vitals."

Mrs. Bagwell shook her head. "Could we wait a couple more minutes?"

"I'll come back later," the nurse agreed.

Dad flipped over a few pages. "Romans 6:23. Read this one."

"For the wages of sin *is* death; but the gift of God *is* eternal life through Jesus Christ our Lord."

"Now Romans 10:9-11."

Mrs. Bagwell focused on the small New Testament. "That if thou shalt confess with thy mouth the Lord Jesus, and shalt believe in thine heart that God hath raised him from the dead, thou shalt be saved. For with the heart man believeth unto righteousness; and with the mouth confession is made unto salvation. For the scripture saith, Whosoever believeth on him shall not be ashamed."

"It's that simple, Mrs. Bagwell. You need to confess to the Lord Jesus that you are a sinner, deserving of hell, and you want to accept Him as your Savior."

Mom hardly dared to breathe, and she felt like she was standing on holy ground as she continued to pray in her heart for Mrs. Bagwell to make the decision. Mrs. Bagwell's eyes filled with tears. "But will God take me since I've lived so much of my life not believing this? Maybe I'm too old."

Dad smiled. "The only time it's too late is after you draw your last breath. As long as you are breathing, the Lord is giving you another opportunity. In second Peter, it says that God's not willing that any should perish, but that all should come to repentance."

Dad and Mom prayed silently, asking the Lord to give Mrs. Bagwell strength to choose Him. "I'm ready, Jim. Tell me what to do."

Dad and Mom knelt by the hospital bed and each took one of her hands. "Go ahead and pray," Dad encouraged. "Tell the Lord Jesus that you are a sinner, and that you are repenting of your sins, and you want to live for Jesus from now on. Ask Him to come into your heart and be your Savior."

Mrs. Bagwell swallowed hard. "Dear God, I hardly know where to begin, but thank You for bringing along the Moodys. They are good people, and more than that, they took the time to talk to me. I see how I have sinned, and really, I've not been a nice woman to be around. Thank You for giving me this opportunity before I might die. I repent of my sin. Please come into my heart and be my Savior. Amen."

Tears trickled down Mrs. Bagwell's cheeks, and her face glowed with delight. "Is there anything else I need to pray?" she asked.

"No," Dad reassured her. "It was perfect, and I'm confident God has heard your prayer."

Mom gently hugged Mrs. Bagwell, and Dad squeezed her hand. "You're now our sister in Christ," Mom said.

"I can't believe it," Mrs. Bagwell sighed. "Jesus is my Savior!"

Chapter 20

The Outcome

"Hi, Mom. It's me. Answer your phone." The strange voice surprised Dad and Mom.

"That's my cell phone," Mrs. Bagwell explained, reaching for her phone on the cart. "My daughter recorded that when I visited her earlier this summer." She answered the phone as the message began to repeat itself. "Hello?"

Mrs. Bagwell's daughter didn't have a quiet voice: "I can't believe you haven't told me before now you were sick. I mean, I AM your daughter. I've been on the phone all evening trying to get a plane ticket, and I'm on my way to the airport right now. I know you've talked about a family who lives near you, and if they're your friends—"

"Cindy—" Mrs. Bagwell interrupted her daughter.

But the voice kept going: "I'm not finished! As I was saying, I'm sure they'll be happy to pick me up. I'll be flying in at 10:37 tonight on Fly'n High Airlines. I'll get some rest and then come right up to see you in the morning. Bye." With that, the phone went dead.

Mrs. Bagwell sighed. "She's not usually so brisk; she must be pretty shook up by what's happening. She didn't even give me her flight number. I could call the airport shuttle to pick Cindy up and take her to my house. It's such an inconvenience for you." Mrs. Bagwell set the phone on the tray.

"We'll work things out; you've told us she lives in Denver, so using that information, the airline name, and the time, we'll figure out the flight number," Dad told her. "Don't worry. What time is your surgery?"

"Eight."

The nurse poked her head in the door. "May I interrupt quickly to check her vitals?"

"Okay." Mrs. Bagwell turned to Mom. "On that keychain I gave you, there's a house key. Cindy will need it, and of course she will drive my car too. Would you please tell your children and Oliver about my being saved? I would myself, but I don't know how long it'll be until I can go home."

"It'll be our delight," Dad assured her. Dad drove Mrs. Bagwell's car and parked it at her house. Then he and Mom traded spots, and a minute later, they pulled into their own driveway. When they walked in the house, Mollie and Maddie were in a corner of the couch, huddled together as Mollie read a book aloud. Grandma was walking around the main part of the house, trying to soothe Melissa's crying. Moses lay contentedly in the swing, and Max and Mitch were reading. "Don't worry, Emily," Grandma assured her. "She only began crying a few minutes ago. Otherwise, she's been fine."

Mom quickly set her purse down. "Thank you for watching the children; I'd love to listen to Dad give the report, but I'm sure the twins are hungry." Mom and Dad brought the twins upstairs, and Dad came back.

"We have news," Dad announced. "Mrs. Bagwell was saved tonight!"

"Really?" Mollie almost squealed and then she began coughing. "We've been praying!" she managed to say.

"Tell us what happened," Grandma settled in Mom's chair.

"First, she told us that she's not been feeling well. I remember when she came for dinner, she mentioned needing to take Pepto-Bismol. Things worsened, and over the last two weeks, she's been feeling really poorly. The doctor thinks she has gallbladder cancer. I guess if a person has gallbladder cancer, there's not much that can be done if it's advanced, and her symptoms indicate that possibility. The doctor's going to do surgery, and he'll know then if it is cancer."

"Oh, that's so sad," Grandma sighed.

"Mr. Delome has witnessed to her. What he said didn't make sense to her. She thought that God would understand that everyone sins, and He'd forgive her. It was a perfect opportunity for me to share the Gospel from Scripture. I explained about God's law, and that when we break the law, we are guilty. The part she was having trouble with is that she felt she hasn't sinned very much compared to others. After we had talked about it and she understood she had broken God's law, she was concerned that she was too old to be saved. Finally, after we reassured her she wasn't, she accepted Jesus as her Lord and Savior. She seemed to have such peace after she prayed."

"I've been praying for her for over a month," Grandma said. "When I talked with her on the 4th of July, I had a heavy burden for her salvation; I'm so excited!"

Max nodded his head. "Mitch and I've been praying for a while too."

"Mom and I are praising the Lord. Her daughter, Cindy, called after that, and she's coming to town. Cindy wants us to get her from the airport around 10:30 tonight. Mrs. Bagwell said she could arrange for a shuttle, but I told her we'd take care of it. I called Grandpa on our way home, and he said you two would be happy to go."

"Of course. What time is Mrs. Bagwell's surgery?"

"Eight o'clock in the morning."

"Do you think she would like us to pray with her before she goes in for surgery?" Grandma wondered. "Grandpa doesn't have to work tomorrow, and he and I could go up there."

"I imagine she would."

"Now I have some news," Grandma said. "Grandpa called me while you were gone, and he told me that our house sold to Dr. Rex!"

"Praise the Lord," Max exclaimed, and the others joined in with their approval.

That night, Mom was awake for several hours taking care of Melissa. In the morning, the children hurried around, doing their normal schedule. Max put cereal on the table. "Poor Mom. It sounds like she had a hard night with Melissa from what Dad said. I heard Melissa crying, but I was able to go back to sleep."

Mitch pulled a gallon of milk from the refrigerator. "I wonder how Mrs. Bagwell is doing."

Mollie washed her hands thoroughly with warm water and soap. "I don't know, but hopefully someone will call us with an update. Dad said he was going to call Mr. Delome on his way to work to tell him about Mrs. Bagwell's salvation."

"Good morning!" Mom surprised them as she walked into the kitchen with Moses. "It looks like you all are busy." She had the baby monitor in her pocket.

"Yes, ma'am," Max responded. "How is Melissa?"

"She's sleeping at least, so I'm hoping she's better."

Mitch nodded. "Are we going to walk?"

"No, since Maddie and Melissa are sleeping, we won't. Moses was sure happy to get up." Mom smiled at him. "You three may ride bikes or do something outside during our walk time. We'll see how Melissa is: I might let Max still have his time with them later this morning. Mollie and Mitch might do their playtime with the babies, too, but Mollie would not be able to hold Moses, since we're trying to protect him from getting sick if possible."

Soon, the children were outside. Max and Mitch pulled their bikes from the garage, and Mollie found a small bucket of sidewalk chalk. She decided she would sketch the hospital where Mrs. Bagwell was having surgery. A few minutes later, Mitch came to an abrupt stop on his bike. "I can tell you're drawing the hospital. You are doing a nice job."

"Where's your helmet?" Max too had stopped, and he looked at Mitch.

"I didn't feel like wearing it because it is so warm," Mitch confessed.

"You need to; we're always supposed to wear a helmet when riding bikes," Max encouraged. "It's for our safety that Dad wants us to wear them."

"I'll do that," Mitch walked off and was soon back with his helmet on.

When their time was up, the children went inside. Maddie sat on the kitchen floor with a bowl of cereal. "Hi Maddie," Max greeted her. "Are you feeling better?"

Maddie sniffled and nodded. "A little bits." She spooned a bite into her mouth. Maddie preferred eating her cereal dry, without any milk added.

"The twins won't have their blanket time," Mom decided, "because Melissa is only now waking up. While you were outside, Grandma Clifton called, and if possible, she'd like Max and Mitch to mow and edge her yard. You may do it this morning at 9:45, since it'll be cooler now than later in the day. We'll skip our meetings, and you will make up math and English this afternoon." Mom brushed Maddie's hair and put it in a ponytail. "You should be back in time to watch the twins, Max."

A little before 9:45, the boys left for Grandma Clifton's. Max pushed the lawn mower, and Mitch carried the trimmer. "Maple wants to come too," Max noticed the golden retriever watching them from the living room window. "Sorry, Maple."

"I wish there was a breeze," Mitch declared. "Maybe Grandma Clifton will have something cold for us to drink when we're through."

"She might, but we brought our water bottles. Mom said we need to drink a lot."

Grandma Clifton was sitting on her porch reading her Bible when the boys arrived. Honey bounded out to greet them and wagged her tail happily. Grandma Clifton smiled. "I hope it's not too hot to do yard work."

"It'll be fine," Max assured her. "I imagine it was hotter than this in Indonesia when you were missionaries."

"That it was."

Mitch hurried to the backyard to pick up dog messes while Max mowed the front yard. As Mitch worked, he prayed for Mrs. Bagwell. *I can't believe we forgot to tell Grandma Clifton about her salvation,* he thought to himself. *She'll be excited.*

An hour and a half later, the yard was in wonderful shape. The grass was mowed, sticks had been picked up, and Mitch's edging job made the yard look tidy. Max rang the doorbell, and Grandma Clifton came out. "Thank you for your work; it looks very nice," she complimented. "The yard wasn't quite ready to be mowed, but I have company coming this weekend, so I wanted everything to look nice."

"Really?" Max said. "Who are your guests?"

"My sister and brother-in-law from Iowa."

"Oh, that's right," Max exclaimed. "They came for Christmas last year."

"Yes, and I felt badly that I didn't bring them over to meet your family. This time I'll make sure to introduce you all." Grandma Clifton stepped back inside. "I mixed up ice-cold lemonade for both of you." She handed them two cups.

"Thank you." Mitch then gulped down the sweet liquid. "Did you hear that Mrs. Bagwell got saved last night?"

"No, I didn't! Please tell me what happened. Was she with you for Bible time?"

"It's quite the story." Max glanced at Mitch.

Grandma Clifton nodded toward the porch. "Do you have a few minutes to sit down and tell me?"

Max checked his watch. "Yes, but we need to be back by 11:30 to watch the twins. We'll tell you the story quickly!" He and Mitch sat on the step while Grandma Clifton settled in her rocking chair.

When they were through, the boys hurried home. Mom, Mollie, and Maddie were in the living room with the twins, and Mom smiled as the boys walked in. "I just talked to Mrs. Bagwell's daughter," she told them. "She said the doctor's report is that it's not cancer, much to everyone's amazement. It's not a problem with her gallbladder but actually with the liver. Something was wrong in the liver, which caused the gallbladder to block up. They've taken care of the blockage, and she should be able to come home in a few days."

"Praise the Lord!" Max exclaimed. "Now we get to see what a saved Mrs. Bagwell is like!"

That night, Melissa woke up crying, and Mom could tell she was feeling miserable. Slipping on her robe, Mom carried Melissa to the living room, hoping to allow Dad and the rest of the family to sleep. Mom decided to sit in a recliner chair that Grandpa and Grandma had given them recently since they were downsizing with their move. Melissa quieted while Mom rocked her. Mom began praying for Mrs. Bagwell, her recovery, and her growth as a new believer. She knew there would be opportunities to encourage her.

Suddenly, a wave of tiredness swept over Mom as Melissa fussed. She wondered how many nights she would be up with Melissa. Not to mention there would be more if Moses came down with it. Her thoughts drifted to her childhood dream of being a nurse. After marrying Dad, she had worked for a year until Max was born. Then it had hit her: being a mommy was important work. No one would ever love her children as much as she did or care for them as she would. With Dad's blessing, she had quit her job. When Max was preschool age, Dad encouraged her to homeschool. Although she had been happy to be at home, the thought of

Melissa quieted while Mom rocked her.

teaching her own children was overwhelming to her. But, as she had prayed about it, the Lord worked mightily in her life, and she had joyfully jumped into homeschooling, seeing the importance of protecting the children from ungodly influences and teaching.

Then Mom's thoughts turned to the sunflowers the girls had grown. The sunflowers received their energy from the sun, and in the early stages of their growth, they were trying to "look" toward the sun's rays. *In the same way,* Mom thought excitedly, *as I keep my focus on Jesus, I receive strength from the Son! But when I cast my eyes on myself, I droop, like the sunflower does when it's heavy with seeds. Thank You, Jesus, for giving me this family,* she whispered. Tears flowed down her face as she realized how blessed she truly was. Instead of feeling sorry for herself, Mom's heart soared with gratefulness.

Summer Days
Not All Fiction!

Tornado sirens—Living in what is called "tornado alley," our sirens usually go off about once a year. We definitely have experienced the excitement of hurrying to the basement when the sirens sound. It was only fitting that this real-life experience be part of the Moodys' life.

I-J-N—Several years ago we arrived in Florida for a conference only a short time after a hurricane had hit the area. Dad announced we would spend part of the day before the conference helping someone clean up. We drove around for a long time before finding a kind, elderly man. He didn't actually need clean up help, but he had a few fix it projects. We have fond memories of helping him.

4th of July—We have enjoyed participating in an annual neighborhood breakfast picnic my brother Nathan and his wife have. It's a wonderful time to interact with neighbors!

Nursing Home Church—Our family has had Sunday morning services in a nursing home for seven years now, and what a blessing it is! One of our elderly friends, who has since gone ahead to Glory, really did hide her pain pills and delay taking them to stay awake for church.

Chocolate Chip Cookies—Years ago, we tasted these delicious cookies and asked for the recipe from friends. We have made them for years, and we still like them! My sisters made countless batches for work men over the two year period our house was being built.

Rosie's Juice—When we were in California giving a conference, we stayed at a hotel, and we had this delicious juice. Upon inquiry, we found out that it was called Rosie's juice, and the rest of the story is true.

Mrs. Bagwell's Situation—Last summer, missionary friends of ours had this health problem happen to their father. I patterned their situation and adapted it to this story for Mrs. Bagwell.

Our Other Resources

Please see the following pages for information on the other books and audios my family offers.

www.Titus2.com   www.HomeschooleCards.com

www.ChorePacks.com   www.PreparingSons.com

www.FamiliesforJesus.com   www.PreparingDaughters.com

The Moody Family Series
Summer (#1), Autumn (#2), Winter (#3),
Spring (#4), and Summer Days (#5)
by Sarah Maxwell

Often parents are concerned about negative examples and role models in books their children are reading. One goal in writing the Moody Series was to eliminate those kinds of examples replacing them with positive, godly ones.

In the books, you'll find the Moodys helping a widowed neighbor, starting small businesses for the children, enjoying a fun night, training their new puppy, homeschooling, Mom experiencing morning sickness, and much more! Woven throughout the books is the Moodys' love for the Lord and their enjoyment of time together. Children (parents too!) will enjoy the Moodys—they'll come away challenged and encouraged.

"My six-year-old son asked Jesus into his heart while we were reading Autumn with the Moodys. *These books are wonderful, heart-warming Christian reading." A mom*

"At last, a Christian book series that is engaging and encourages my children to love Jesus more and bless their family and friends." A mom

To order or for information visit: www.Titus2.com.
Or call: (913) 772-0392.

Managers of Their Homes

A Practical Guide to Daily Scheduling for Christian Homeschool Families

by Steven and Teri Maxwell

A homeschool mother's greatest challenge may be "getting it all done." *Managers of Their Homes* offers solutions! Responses by families who have read *Managers of Their Homes* and utilized the Scheduling Kit indicate the almost unbelievable improvements they have realized.

Step-by-step instructions and a unique Scheduling Kit make the setting up of a daily schedule easily achievable for any homeschooling family. Who wouldn't like to accomplish more and have time left over?

How does one schedule school time? Are you struggling with keeping up in areas such as laundry, dishes, or housekeeping? Do you feel stressed over the busyness of your days or not accomplishing all you want? It doesn't matter whether you have one child or twelve, this book will help you to plan your daily schedule.

Managers of Their Homes sets a firm biblical foundation for scheduling, in addition to discussing scheduling's numerous benefits. Chapter after chapter is filled with practical suggestions for efficient, workable ways to schedule a homeschooling family's days. Thirty real-life schedules in the Appendix give valuable insight into creating a personalized schedule. Also included is a special chapter by Steve for homeschool dads.

"My schedule has given me back my sanity!! I can't believe the way my life has changed since implementing a schedule." Tracy

"Making and using a schedule has helped me, and there were people who thought I was hopeless!" Sheri

"I had read almost every organizational book there was, and I still couldn't get to where I wanted to be until I applied this method!" Corrie

To order or for information visit: www.Titus2.com.
Or call: (913) 772-0392.

Managers of Their Chores

A Practical Guide to Children's Chores

by Steven and Teri Maxwell

In the same way that *Managers of Their Homes* helped tens of thousands of moms "get it all done," *Managers of Their Chores* helps families conquer the chore battle. The book and included ChorePack system have the potential to revolutionize the way your family accomplishes chores. Whether you are chore challenged or a seasoned chore warrior, you will gain motivation and loads of practical advice on implementing a stress-free chore system.

Managers of Their Chores comes with all the ChorePack materials needed for four children, including ChorePacks, chore card paper, and a ChorePack holder. In the appendix of the book, you will find a chore library with more than 180 chores listed, forms for photocopying, and sample chore assignments from eight families.

Use *Managers of Their Chores* to help your family achieve a chore system that is as stress free as possible. This book puts tools into parents' hands that will allow them to be successful in a chore system with their children. From preschoolers to teens, each person can be a contributing member of the family while gaining lifelong personal benefits that prepare him for life.

"I can't believe how much time we have gained in our days now that we have our ChorePack system in place." A mom

"Its simplicity and ease of use encouraged independence and accountability at a young age." A mom

"It gave you visuals, explained the whys, needs, and benefits of chores, plus giving a system for implementing them. The book walked you through the process very clearly one step at a time with explanation of what to do and why." A mom

To order or for information visit: www.Titus2.com.
Or call: (913) 772-0392.

Managers of Their Schools
A Practical Guide to Homeschooling

by Steven and Teri Maxwell

Have you ever wanted to sit down with an experienced homeschooling couple and ask them every question you could think of about homeschooling? *Managers of Their Schools: A Practical Guide to Homeschooling* is the next best thing. With eight children and twenty-three years as a homeschooling family, the Maxwells share their answers to the questions they are frequently asked.

This book is filled with practical information regarding how one family homeschools, what they use, why they do what they do, and how it all works for them. Steve and Teri set down the details of homeschooling in a real-life family, from how they make curricula decisions to whether their children take tests.

After spending their first twelve years searching for a homeschool method that met their Scriptural and educational criteria, they finally began using Christian textbooks and have never wanted to change direction again. In this book, Steve and Teri share the benefits their family has gained from using textbooks, and they refute the reasons many will say homeschoolers should not use textbooks.

There is a chapter written by the four adult Maxwell children sharing some of their homeschool thoughts, particularly with regard to using Christian textbooks. The appendix of *Managers of Their Schools* includes ten of the Maxwell's school schedules, several assignment sheets, a listing of the school curricula and resources the Maxwells personally use, plus coupon codes for discounts on some of them.

Whether or not you use the same method to home educate as the Maxwells, you will find a wealth of tried-and-true, daily-life homeschool information. Make your homeschooling journey that much easier, more efficient, and more joyful by learning from a family who has already walked the path.

"I have learned so much from the book. The time I will save in planning for this school year is astronomical!" A mom

**To order or for information visit: www.Titus2.com.
Or call: (913) 772-0392.**

Keeping Our Children's Hearts

Our Vital Priority

By Steven and Teri Maxwell

Written for parents of young children to teenagers, this book shares the joys and outcomes of our vital priority—keeping our children's hearts. Rebellion and immorality are common among teens even within the Christian community. Does Scripture offer any path of hope for more than this for our children? What can parents do to direct their children toward godliness rather than worldliness? When does this process begin? What is the cost?

Steve and Teri Maxwell believe the key factors in raising children in the nurture and admonition of the Lord (Ephesians 6:4) are whether or not the parents have their children's hearts and what they are doing with those hearts. *Keeping Our Children's Hearts* offers direction and encouragement on this critically important topic.

Included in this book is a chapter co-authored by three of the adult Maxwell children concerning their thoughts, feelings, experiences, and outcomes of growing up in a home where their parents wanted to keep their hearts. There are also questions at the end of each chapter, which are thought provoking and helpful.

"The most complete and most balanced book I have read on how to raise children who won't rebel!" Dr. S. M. Davis

"This book is making me rethink what my purpose as a Christian, mother, and homeschooler should be." A mom

"The Scripture and its experiential application was encouraging and refreshing." A dad

"It truly is my top child rearing book now. You have brought together all the issues we have been striving to understand and achievements we hope to make with our children." A mom

To order or for information visit: www.Titus2.com.
Or call: (913) 772-0392.

Homeschooling with a Meek and Quiet Spirit

by Teri Maxwell

The desire of a homeschooling mother's heart is to have a meek and quiet spirit instead of discouragement, fear, and anger.

Because Teri Maxwell, a mother of eight, has walked the homeschooling path since 1985, she knows first-hand the struggle for a meek and quiet spirit. The memories from her early homeschooling years of often being worried and angry rather than having a meek and quiet spirit are not what she would like them to be.

Will your journey toward a meek and quiet spirit be completed upon finding the perfect spelling curriculum or deciding which chores your child should be doing? Perhaps the answer lies on a different path.

In these pages, Teri offers practical insights into gaining a meek and quiet spirit that any mom can apply to her individual circumstances. She transparently shares the struggles God has brought her through and what He has shown her during these many homeschooling years.

As you read *Homeschooling with a Meek and Quiet Spirit,* you will discover the heart issues that will gently lead you to a meek and quiet spirit. Come along and join Teri as you seek the Lord to homeschool with a meek and quiet spirit!

A study guide is also available.

"This is one of the best, most helpful, encouraging, and empathetic books I've read during my 5 years of homeschooling." A mom

"I wish all moms, regardless of their school choice, could read Homeschooling with a Meek and Quiet Spirit." *Kathy*

"It is not just for homeschooling moms, but any mom who wants to be the best mom she can be. It was challenging, enlightening, and encouraging." A mom

**To order or for information visit: www.Titus2.com.
Or call: (913) 772-0392.**

Preparing Sons

to Provide for a Single-Income Family

By Steven Maxwell

In today's world of two-income families, preparing a son to provide for a single-income family seems an overwhelming task. Christian parents will find it helpful to have a purpose and plan as they raise sons who will one day be responsible for supporting a family.

Steve Maxwell presents the groundwork for preparing your son to be a wage-earning adult. He gives practical suggestions and direction to parents for working with their sons from preschool age all the way to adulthood. You will be challenged to evaluate your own life and the example you are setting for your son.

As the father of eight children, five of them now wage-earning adults, Steve has gained valuable experience he openly shares with other parents. Learn these principles from a dad whose twenty-four-year-old homeschooled son purchased a home debt free a year before his marriage, and whose second son has done the same. Steve explains how it is possible for parents, with a willing commitment, to properly prepare their sons to provide for a single-income family.

"You are dealing with topics that no one I know of has dealt with as thoroughly and practically as you have." Dr. S. M. Davis

"Preparing Sons was a big blessing to my husband. All you ladies should get a copy for your husband and every church library needs one." Shelly

"I highly recommend the book for those of you who have not read it. I really appreciate all the obvious prayer, effort, and experience that went into making this book. The Lord is using it for His Glory in our family." Les

Preparing Sons is available in paperback or unabridged audiobook.

To order or for information visit: www.Titus2.com.
Or call: (913) 772-0392.

Men's Book
(Title to be announced)

by Steve Maxwell

Available Fall 2009

Most men today would say that they are under time pressure. In the midst of their busyness, there are key aspects of their daily lives that suffer such as their relationships with the Lord, with their wives, and with their children. They aren't keeping up with their normal responsibilities. They are tired, stressed, and struggling.

Author, Titus2 ministry founder, engineer, and CEO of two small businesses, Steve Maxwell has much experience in time management. He shares Biblical truths that will allow a man to gain control over the time pressures that he is facing. Steve discusses practical aspects of time management that put a man on a path to being able to keep up with the various demands on his time. In this book you will learn how it is possible to go from pressure, chaos, and stress to peace, order, and productivity.

To order or for information visit: www.Titus2.com.
Or call: (913) 772-0392.

To The Parents

Do you want to be challenged in your walk with the Lord and in your responsibilities as a parent? Steve and Teri write free, monthly encouragement articles called the Dad's and Mom's Corners. Sign up on our website, www.Titus2.com, call us at (913) 772-0392, or e-mail: managers@Titus2.com

---

Just Around the Corner

Encouragement and Challenge
for Christian Dads and Moms, Volumes 1 and 2
(Volume 3 Coming Soon!)

By Steven and Teri Maxwell

 *Just Around the Corner* (Volumes 1 and 2) is a compilation of Steve and Teri Maxwell's monthly Dad's and Mom's Corners. Steve's writing will challenge dads in their role as the spiritual head of the family. Teri's writing addresses many aspects of daily life that often frustrate or discourage a mom.

You will find the Mom's Corners grouped together in the front of the book and the Dad's Corners in the back. The Corners are all indexed so that you can read the ones relating to a specific topic you are interested in, if you so choose.

Topics addressed in *Just Around the Corner* include anger, child training, dads being the leaders of their families, depression, influencing children's spiritual outcome, homeschooling, husband/wife relationships, parenting, and much more!

With five of the Maxwell children now adults, Steve and Teri write from the perspective of having seen the truth of God's Word put into practice. At the same time, they are still in the trenches homeschooling three children.

"The Maxwells are so encouraging and down to earth. I had been feeling down about some negative behavior in my children, things in my marriage, homeschooling, and the list goes on. This book has helped me to regain my focus and carry on to what God has called me to do." Michelle

"The Lord has used Volume 1 *this week to really speak to my heart. It is amazing how He put the order of the articles just the way I need them right now!" A mom*

To order or for information visit: www.Titus2.com.
Or call: (913) 772-0392.

Manager of His Home

Helping Your Wife Succeed As She Manages Your Home

By Steve Maxwell

Do you desire to know what practical, spiritual headship actually means, and does your wife long for this? How do you lead and still allow her to manage the home?

In this audio session you will be given real-life, biblical suggestions for how you can support and facilitate your wife in her role as a homeschooling mom.

"I would recommend this message to others because it provided plenty of practical, daily examples of how to lead the family." A dad

Encouragement for the Homeschool Family

By the Maxwells

Encouragement for the Homeschool Family is an eight-session audio seminar which will encourage, exhort, and equip homeschooling families. Included in the album: *The Homeschooling Family–Building a Vision, Managers of Their Homes, Manager of His Home, Loving Your Husband, Sports–Friend or Foe, Anger–Relationship Poison, Experiencing the Joy of Young Womanhood,* and *Success or Failure* (for young men).

(Single titles are also available separately: **www.Titus2.com**)

To order or for information visit: www.Titus2.com.
Or call: (913) 772-0392.

Feed My Sheep

A Practical Guide to Daily Family Bible Time
by Steve Maxwell

Tried them and failed? Never tried because you knew it would be too big of a battle? No time for them even if you wanted to? Do any of these questions describe your experience with family Bible time? This two CD set is highly motivational and practical.

In the first CD, Steve Maxwell gives practical advice for achieving success with family Bible time. He reveals the secret that he guarantees will work

The second CD will help you gain ideas on how simple it is to implement a family Bible time as you join the Maxwell family for two of theirs. You'll feel like you're right at home with Steve as you listen to him lead his family in their time in the Word. You will see how easy it is to lead your family in the most important time of the day.

Join Steve, father of eight, as he shares about the Maxwells' favorite part of their day. We pray you'll come away with an excitement for the daily feeding of your family from God's Word!

Anger–Relationship Poison
by Steve & Teri Maxwell

Homeschooling families have a heart's desire to raise godly children. However, it seems that anger is found in many homeschooling parents, and it can undermine all the hours invested in positive teaching. Have you noticed how certain levels of anger are accepted and justified? Is a little anger beneficial? Do you have difficulty controlling your anger? Is a harsh tone in your voice anger? Are you discouraged by the anger in your life and in your home? Steve and Teri will encourage you on this universally needed topic as they share from God's Word and personal testimonies.

To order or for information visit: www.Titus2.com.
Or call: (913) 772-0392.

Experiencing the Joy of Young Womanhood

By Sarah Maxwell

Sarah explores aspects of a young woman's life that lead to true joy. It all starts with the foundation—your relationship with Jesus Christ. She delves into hindrances to joy as well as practical aspects of it. Plenty of personal testimonies from Sarah's life are sprinkled into the session.

Success or Failure— Where Are You Headed?

By Christopher Maxwell

Homeschooled young men have incredible potential for success in their lives—both spiritually and vocationally. There are tragic pitfalls that might appear innocuous on the surface to be avoided. In addition there are basic elements crucial for success in the spiritual world and in the business world. This session explores how the different aspects of a young man's life will affect his future.

Sports—Friend or Foe? by Steve Maxwell

Homeschooling families are heavily involved in sports. What are the parents' goals in having their children participate in organized sports? Are these goals being met? Are the children better or worse by being one of the team? Steve shares the Maxwells' experience on sports as well as incorporating data from a large on-line survey that he conducted regarding Christian families and sports.

To order or for information visit: www.Titus2.com.
Or call: (913) 772-0392.

Family Evangelism–
Effectively Sharing Christ & Loving It
By Christopher Maxwell

Charles Spurgeon once said, "Have you no wish for others to be saved? Then you are not saved yourself. Be sure of that." While many believers might have a deep desire to see others saved, they aren't actively sharing their faith. From overcoming fear, to studying how Jesus witnessed to the lost, to the missing ingredient in modern evangelism, this session is designed to equip, motivate, and encourage you! You'll hear real life examples that resulted from everyday opportunities—opportunities that you can also experience. Transform your desire to share into reality.

How to Start and Run Your Own Home Business (For Young People)
by Christopher & Sarah Maxwell

During your teen years, homeschool students have incredible opportunities to start, run, and build successful businesses. You will not only be earning income but also learning invaluable life skills. In this practical session, given by a brother and sister team, Christopher and Sarah Maxwell share how you can start your own business. The session will cover issues such as: What type of business should you start or avoid? What are the legal and tax ramifications? What skills do you need and how do you acquire them? Plus much more. You'll come away with specific ideas—and hopefully a big dose of motivation—to start your own business! Don't waste your teen years—do something beneficial!

To order or for information visit: www.Titus2.com.
Or call: (913) 772-0392.

The Homeschooling Family—Building a Vision
by Steve & Teri Maxwell

Whether new or experienced homeschoolers, this motivational and practical session helps a family attain their heartfelt goals for raising and educating their children. Doubts, discouragement, and burnout can easily shipwreck the family that doesn't know "where they are going." What is it that keeps a family homeschooling through a mom's feelings of being overwhelmed, a child with a rebellious spirit, or a house full of babies and toddlers?

Together, Steve and Teri share in this session how they moved from homeschooling for convenience (we'll try it a year and see how it goes) to homeschooling forever. They will give you concrete examples from homeschooling struggles they have experienced and how they made it through. With five adult children whom they homeschooled and three more children who are currently being homeschooled, they have the experience to know how to keep on while still being in the trenches of day to day homeschooling.

Loving Your Husband
by Teri Maxwell

This is an incredible session every woman should listen to. It is easy for a mom to become consumed with children and day-to-day life. This leaves the opportunity for creating a huge gap in her relationship with the key person in her life—her husband. Don't damage or lose that special relationship with your husband but rather develop and strengthen it.

To order or for information visit: www.Titus2.com.
Or call: (913) 772-0392.